Advance Praise for *Now We're Cooking*

"Anyone who follows @acooknamedmatt knows his food is bold, creative, fearless, and instantly irresistible. In *Now We're Cooking*, Matt brings that same energy to a collection of laid-back, flavor-packed recipes that build confidence and deliver every time."

—J. Kenji López-Alt, author of *The Food Lab* and *The Wok*

"Stunning, mouthwatering, and, at times, audaciously vulnerable, *Now We're Cooking* doesn't just show us who Broussard is. It proves that food is sometimes the best way to discover who we are."

—Joanne Lee Molinaro, author of *The Korean Vegan*

"Matt is more than a cook; he's an innovative, passionate creator in film and an expert chef. Driven by passion for his craft, he inspires his community to strive for perfection in flavor through visual storytelling."

—Shereen Pavlides, bestselling author and creator of *Cooking with Shereen*

"In a world of shortcut cooking, Matt stays true to the craft. He's managed to bottle the cheat codes of a high-end restaurant kitchen and fuse them with the warmth of home cooking. This book is a great tool for anyone who wants to stop just 'making food' and start truly understanding flavor."

—Lisa Nguyen (@its.lisanguyen)

"Matt's recipes in *Now We're Cooking* are so undeniably exciting, sexy, and downright delicious that I'm jealous he can't be my private chef. His authenticity, love of his family, and passion for his craft build the sense of trust that we all want when following recipes. And I'm making his tacos."

—Ryan Nordheimer (@ryannordheimer)

"Matt brings restaurant-level flavor into the home kitchen with bold techniques, simple ingredients, and no-nonsense cooking. This book is packed with recipes that hit hard (particularly our flying noodles on page 117)."

—Vincent Yeow Lim (@dimsimlim)

"I rarely cook anything outside Korean food, but when I do, it's always Matt's recipes."

—Chris Cho (@chefchrischo)

"Matt is the definition of comfort food done with intention. His technique is clean, his flavors hit home, and every dish feels like something you want to go back to again and again. After years of cooking beside him, I can say this: he's a real one. A true friend who doesn't quite keep his talent small, and this book proves it."

—Shota Nakajima

"Matthew is great, I just smile every time I see his videos; been rocking with him since the beginning of TikTok."

—Jimmy O. Yang

NOW WE'RE COOKING

Fs
GOLD
Spri

NOW WE'RE COOKING

All-Purpose, Laid-Back Recipes

MATTHEW BROUSSARD
@acooknamedmatt
with Erin Ryan and Rick Rodgers

Photography by Sarah Flotard

Simon Element
New York Amsterdam/Antwerp London Toronto Sydney/Melbourne New Delhi

For you. Thank you
for supporting me on
this wild, wild wave.

Table of

Contents

Introduction

Not until your belly button reaches the stove.

For years those words stood between me and the cooktop, where bacon came from. I watched as my grandma—Grand, to me—fried the fatty slab to semi-soggy perfection and then cracked an egg in the grease. It was a mystery to me, how she got the white on top.

Basting an egg was the first thing she taught me when I was finally tall enough.

I grew up in Grand's kitchen in Southmost. The old neighborhood is on the very tip of Brownsville on the very tip of Texas, just five miles from the Mexican border. *Tortillerias* are everywhere, and a fresh stack meant my favorite snacks. Warm corn tortillas rolled with salt, crispy chicken flautas with tons of sour cream, and the almost-quesadilla Grand made by toasting a tortilla in oil, melting Colby-Jack on top, and folding it once with a pinch of salt.

Then and now, from top left: With Grand in her Brownsville kitchen; at the Palace Kitchen grill with mentor Nathan Crave; Palace's back stairs in two different eras.

Sundays were for barbacoa tacos at home, extra special when my ma did her crock-pot *lengua*. My aunts had their own specialties. Aunt Sheri's *sandwichón* made her a legend at all the baby showers. Picture layers of white bread and chicken salad topped with cream cheese frosting, nuts, pineapple rings, and cherries, served with a side of fucking Lay's potato chips. So good.

My foundation as a cook came from these women. But Grand taught me the most, about food and everything else.

Brownsville is weird. Isolated. If you look on a map, there's a long stretch of nothing between civilization and the Rio Grande Valley on that triangle point of Texas. It's like its own country. Grand told me about the outside world, and the family stories no one else knew. She took me to every park and to the zoo so many times I knew all the animal names by heart. She got me my first Game Boy, a lime-green beauty that still functions. While my ma worked two jobs to support us, Grand let me be a kid.

And she is the reason I don't have the full Brownsville culture in me. She wasn't from there. Grand is full-blooded Syrian—born to Syrian parents in Santiago, Chile, then raised in San Diego, California, by her mom and Filipino stepdad. She came to the Rio Grande Valley because of my grandpa, who grew up in the nearby town of Matamoros. That's why she made Mexican food so much. Also, because it was delicious.

Grand loved Italian cooking, too. This mix of flavors lived in her food: dolmas and rice noodles, enchiladas and pizza burgers. Whatever she made, I wanted to make. Because I was curious, and because I was a mixed-race kid of a single mom living on the border. Food was how I understood myself.

It still is, and it's the best way I've found to understand other people.

I'd been cooking for eight years by the time I got my first restaurant job when I was 16, on the line at a Mexican place where everyone spoke Spanish but me. Then it was a chain steakhouse, touristy spots on South Padre Island, a country club, and finally a tavern I opened with someone else's money. I was getting somewhere, but what I really needed was to get out of Texas.

I had no clue where I wanted to go, so I focused on who I wanted to learn from. Following the restaurant scene, I kept seeing Tom Douglas's name. He was a godfather of Pacific Northwest cuisine with a bunch of Seattle restaurants, and his food made sense to me. It was all about the place—fish from the Pacific, mushrooms from the Olympic Peninsula, berries and cheeses from local farms—showcased in ways that were smart and surprising without trying too hard. He took familiar dishes everybody loved and made them exciting.

Of all Tom's restaurants, Palace Kitchen spoke to me the most. You could get a perfect steak at 1 a.m., or a plate of Alpine nachos with pickled fish. The menu changed constantly because Tom's chefs had creative freedom. They'd all been in the job forever, beat to hell. That is what makes you better. So, as a 21-year-old who'd never really been anywhere, I took my shot.

That involved getting a recommendation. Not from a chef. From a senator.

I happened to know Texas State Senator Eddie Lucio. I met him working at the country club, and he was friends with this circle of old guys I hung out with at the Brownsville Starbucks. These were characters who'd seen shit and knew shit and gave me advice about *everything*. I learned to work my connections, and Eddie was game to help me.

His letter and my crazy résumé were enough to get me an interview at Palace Kitchen. So I moved to Seattle, sight unseen. The city was awesome. My apartment . . . let's just say bedbugs woke me up at 3 a.m. the first night, and they were so bad I tried sleeping in the bathtub with my cat. A few hours later, after scrolling on Craigslist with all my things in my car, I found a new place and crashed on the floor. Not the best night before my *stage* at Palace.

I had $500 and no backup plan. There was a voice in my head, though. One I'd been listening to my whole life. If I told Grand I wanted to build rockets on Mars, she'd be like, "Cool, go do it."

I went right into the fire on Palace's grill during Friday service. We were rocking and I got burned. It was hard. Everything. At the end of the night, my chef Dezi Bonow hired me and told me I had a bright future in Seattle.

When I had a chance to unpack my suitcase, I found this Post-it note tucked inside.

MY DEAR GRANDSON, FORGE YOUR OWN PATH, ANYTHING IS POSSIBLE

I learned a stupid amount over six years with Tom's group, ending with me roving fifteen of his restaurants as a tournant while doing pop-ups on the side. But teaching is what hooked me into the life I have

FORGE YOUR OWN PATH,
ANYTHING IS POSSIBLE

now. Tom has a cooking school called the Hot Stove Society, for home cooks at every level who want to go deeper. Teaching classes there—seeing students' faces when they realized how to caramelize onions properly or make restaurant-level pie crust—lit me up. Even the basics blew minds, and I wanted to show way more people how much was within reach.

When the pandemic closed Tom's restaurants and shoved me online, I found my sweet spot doing just that. Back where I started, cooking at home with the same joy I had as an 8-year-old, but with real know-how. I already had an audience on social media, and the more I made the food I loved, the more it grew.

Now I get to connect with people everywhere through food. Through *my* food. It's a mix hugely influenced by my family, whether we're talking blood or the brothers and sisters I've found in every kind of kitchen you can imagine, from Michelin-starred to sketchy grills at the park. Everything I share is about taking the mystery out of cooking, just like Grand did for me.

I know why food tastes better at restaurants, and I'm here with the cheat codes—the insights and tricks that will help you build not just flavor, but trust. Trust to leave stuff alone in the pan without poking it every other second. Trust to season heavily and to cook with high heat. You'll learn why it can be good to almost burn your vegetables; how to blend hot ingredients without exploding them all over yourself; when to go canned instead of fresh; and what makes for the best texture in everything from pizza crust to fried chicken. You'll also find the secret to making noodles fly.

However inexperienced you are as a cook, you can make a good dish. Just remember that food is food. Everything breaks down to a bunch of components and moves anyone can learn, even if it takes a minute to get comfy and be proud of what you made. Get in there with your hands. Do the reps and have faith. And fun. That's what cooking was to me from my first day manning Grand's stove in Southmost. She inspired me and gave me the confidence to try things, fuck up, and get better, and I'm hoping to do that for you.

Grand's words from that old Post-it are tattooed on my arm, because she was right. Anything is possible. The cookbook in your hands is the sweetest proof.

I hope it's all bangers for you. Either way, you should make my tacos.

Chapter 1

Apps

PACIFICO

Michelada Snapper Ceviche with Avocado

Where I grew up, right on the tip of Texas on the Gulf of Mexico, people eat a lot of fish and drink a lot of micheladas. They go together so well because the michelada is a Bloody Mary made with beer, and seafood likes the spicy heat of a Bloody, the acidity of tomato and lime, and the crispness of a light lager. When the base is Clamato juice (and it should be), you also get that briny depth from the clam broth. The whole mix gives you a perfect marinade to make ceviche, which I do here with slightly sweet red snapper, the king of the Gulf. The recipe also can be made with oysters on the half shell (see the variation), a sexy appetizer for a special meal.

Serves 6

Ceviche

1 (12-ounce) bottle Mexican lager beer (such as Corona or Pacifico)

1 cup clam-tomato juice (such as Clamato) or tomato juice

½ cup tequila añejo (see Takeaways)

¼ cup fresh lime juice

2 tablespoons minced shallot

2 tablespoons soy sauce

1 tablespoon Worcestershire sauce

1 tablespoon gochugaru (Korean chili flakes)

1 tablespoon guajillo powder

1 tablespoon minced cilantro stems (save the leaves for serving)

1 serrano chile, cut into thin rounds (including seeds)

1 pound skinless snapper fillets, cut into ½-inch pieces

Seasoned Salt

1 tablespoon kosher salt

1½ teaspoons gochugaru (Korean chili flakes)

1½ teaspoons sumac

To Serve

2 ripe Hass avocados, pitted and cut into ½-inch dice

Cilantro leaves

Thinly sliced red onion

Lime rounds

Saltine crackers

Make the ceviche: Whisk the beer, clam-tomato juice, tequila, lime juice, shallot, soy sauce, Worcestershire sauce, gochugaru, guajillo powder, cilantro stems, and serrano in a medium bowl. Add the snapper, cover tightly with plastic wrap, and refrigerate until well chilled and the snapper is turning opaque, about 1½ hours (the sweet spot between a sushi-like inside and firm).

Make the seasoned salt: Mix the salt, gochugaru, and sumac in a small bowl to combine.

To serve: Drain away most of the marinade from the snapper, keeping about ⅓ cup in the bowl. Gently mix in the avocado. Transfer the ceviche to a serving bowl and sprinkle with some seasoned salt followed by the cilantro leaves. Fill a larger bowl with crushed ice. Nestle the bowl with the ceviche in the ice, garnish with the red onion and lime rounds, and serve immediately with the crackers.

Oysters Michelada:

Serves 4

Shuck 2 dozen of your favorite oysters and place the oyster meat in a small bowl with their brine. Reserve the shells. Add the marinade to the bowl with the oysters and refrigerate for 1½ hours.

Before serving, rub a lime wedge along the edges of each shell. Sprinkle the seasoned salt on the shells to give them salted rims. Fill four wide soup bowls with crushed ice. Slip a marinated oyster and some of the marinade into each shell. Nestle six oysters into each bowl and garnish with lime wedges. Serve immediately.

TAKEAWAYS

- Tequila añejo has been aged in oak barrels to give it a deeper flavor than younger blanco tequila. Because of the spiciness of the marinade, the richer añejo allows the tequila taste to come through. And it doesn't need to be expensive to have that depth.
- Other top-quality fish, like tuna or halibut, can be substituted for the snapper.

Almost Grandma's Dolmas

My family always joked that Grand stuffed everything—from cabbage and bell peppers to jalapeños. It must have been her Syrian roots, because stuffed foods are big in that cuisine. I loved her dolmas, aka stuffed grape leaves. They were super-lemony, cooked in the juice that I squeezed. Her filling wasn't exactly authentic, and you should feel free to play around with the ingredients, too (dill, dried currants, pine nuts—you get the idea). Because grape leaves vary in size, the filling amount may not be an exact match. The average is about 1 tablespoon, but depending on the leaf, you may need a little more or less for the perfect bite.

Serves 4 to 6

Filling

⅓ cup duck fat or extra virgin olive oil

1 medium yellow onion, finely chopped

4 cloves garlic, crushed into a paste (see Takeaways)

2 tablespoons dried oregano

1 teaspoon Aleppo pepper or ½ teaspoon crushed hot red pepper

1 pound ground lamb or beef chuck

2 cups cooked long-grain rice, preferably jasmine

2 tablespoons soy sauce

½ teaspoon kosher salt

¼ teaspoon freshly ground black pepper

Dolmas

1 (32-ounce) jar grape leaves in brine, rinsed and drained (see Takeaways)

⅓ cup fresh lemon juice

Plain Greek yogurt, for dipping

TAKEAWAYS

- You don't need a garlic press in your life when you have a large chef's knife. When garlic paste is called for, finely chop the garlic on a cutting board. Add a pinch of kosher salt and keep chopping until the garlic is minced. Now place the flat side of the knife over the garlic and press and smear it on the board until it's paste. Scrape it up and use as needed.
- Brined grape leaves are sold in jars at Middle Eastern markets, online, and at some supermarkets.
- You can use collard greens or Swiss chard in place of the grape leaves. Cut into pieces about 4 inches square (avoiding the thick stems). Blanch the greens or the chard as directed for the fresh grape leaves, below.
- Grand would blanch her own fresh leaves after we picked them from my great-grandma's tree in San Diego, and if you have access to some, do the same: First, rinse the leaves well and trim any thick stems. Bring a large pot of salted water to a full boil over high heat. Add the leaves and cook until barely tender, 1 to 2 minutes. Drain in a colander and transfer to a bowl of ice water to cool completely. Drain again and pat the leaves dry with paper or kitchen towels.

Make the filling: Heat the duck fat in a large skillet over medium heat. Add the onion and garlic and cook, stirring occasionally, until the onions are translucent, about 4 minutes. Stir in the oregano and Aleppo pepper and cook until fragrant, about 30 seconds. Add the lamb and increase the heat to medium-high. Cook, stirring occasionally and breaking up the meat with the side of a spoon until the meat is no longer pink, about 8 minutes. Stir in the rice, soy sauce, salt, and black pepper. Pour off the excess fat, if desired. Transfer to a bowl and let cool. Cover and refrigerate until chilled, at least 2 hours or up to 1 day.

Stuff and cook the dolmas: Separate the grape leaves and identify 3 dozen of the largest intact leaves for stuffing, setting aside the smaller or torn leaves for layering. Snip off the stems. Place a large grape leaf on the work surface, stem end facing you. Put about a heaping tablespoon of the filling in the bottom third of the leaf. Fold in the right and left sides to cover the filling. Bring up the bottom of the leaf to cover the filling, and give the leaf a slight tuck under the filling to tighten, then roll it up, tucking in the sides as you go for a tight roll. Transfer to a baking sheet. Continue with the remaining filling and large leaves.

Line the bottom of a large, heavy skillet with a single layer of the reserved smaller leaves. Arrange half of the stuffed leaves in a spoke pattern in the skillet. Cover with another single layer of the reserved smaller leaves, then arrange another layer of stuffed leaves on top. Mix the lemon juice and ⅔ cup water and pour over the leaves. Place a plate or flat pot lid on top of the layered grape leaves to weigh them down slightly.

Bring to a simmer over medium heat. Reduce the heat to low and cover tightly with the skillet lid, leaving the plate in place. Simmer until the grape leaves are heated through, about 15 minutes. Uncover and let stand for 5 minutes.

Transfer the dolmas to a platter. Serve warm or cooled, with the yogurt for dipping.

Chile-Pickled Deviled Eggs

Eggs are fun. Deviling them is something I've done a ton, and it's not hard to get creative with this staple of American cooking. Win your next picnic by lightly pickling the hard-boiled whites in a jalapeño-infused brine then filling each with a bright yellow swirl spiked with guajillo chile. Because I like my snacks cute *and* hot.

Serves 8

12 large eggs

1½ cups unseasoned rice vinegar

1 tablespoon sugar

1 jalapeño chile, cut into thin rounds, seeds included

Kosher salt

⅓ cup mayonnaise (such as Kewpie)

2 tablespoons sour cream

½ teaspoon ground guajillo chile, plus more for garnish

¼ teaspoon dry mustard

Finely chopped fresh chives or scallions, for garnish

Flaky salt, for garnish

Extra virgin olive oil, for serving

Add about 3 inches water to a large saucepan or Dutch oven, enough to cover the eggs in a single layer (if you're using a medium saucepan, cook the eggs in two batches of six to avoid crowding). Cover and bring to a boil over high heat. Using a slotted spoon, carefully add each egg to the water. Reduce the heat and simmer for 12 minutes. Using the slotted spoon, transfer the eggs to a bowl of ice water. Let stand for 10 minutes to thoroughly chill the eggs.

Crack and peel the eggs, then cut each in half from top to bottom. Transfer the yolks to a small bowl, cover tightly with plastic wrap, and refrigerate. Transfer the egg white halves to a shallow glass or ceramic baking dish.

Bring 1½ cups water, the vinegar, sugar, jalapeño, and 2 teaspoons salt to a boil in a medium saucepan over high heat, stirring to dissolve the sugar. Pour over the egg whites. Let cool to tepid, about 1 hour. Cover tightly with plastic wrap and refrigerate for 1 to 2 hours.

Using a slotted spoon, transfer the pickled whites to paper towels to drain. Rub the yolks through a coarse wire sieve into a small bowl. Add the mayonnaise, sour cream, ground guajillo, and mustard and mash well with a silicone or rubber spatula. Using a teaspoon, stuff the whites with the filling. (Or put the filling in a pastry bag fitted with a large star tip, such as Ateco #826, and use it to fill the whites.)

Arrange the deviled eggs on a serving platter. Sprinkle with additional guajillo powder, chives, and flaky salt. Drizzle with the oil and serve chilled.

TAKEAWAYS

- Chop up any leftover pickled egg whites and yolks with a little more mayonnaise, if needed, to make it spreadable for a great egg salad sandwich.
- Why are some boiled eggs easy to peel, and others are assholes? The easy ones are older. They've had a chance to sit and get more porous and less acidic, meaning more air between the shell and the membrane of the egg. For easier peeling, don't boil the eggs you just bought.

Pimiento Cheese with Soft Pretzels

Pimiento cheese is a Southern obsession you may not have tried. But if you've ever used paprika, you know the sweet nip of the aromatic pimiento pepper. Its pickled bite and hot red color are needed in this creamy cheesiness, which is good with store-bought crackers or flatbread, but the pretzel is the point. And if you pickle your own peppers for this, you'll have extra around to wake up fancy egg sandwiches and microwave burritos alike.

Serves 8; makes about 1½ cups cheese sauce

Pimiento Cheese

4 ounces cream cheese, at room temperature

1½ cups shredded sharp cheddar cheese (see Takeaways)

½ cup mayonnaise

⅓ cupchopped drained Pickled Red Peppers (page 226) or drained store-bought chopped pimiento (see Takeaways)

Pretzels

1 No-Knead Pizza Dough (page 242), made at least 10 hours before baking

Unbleached all-purpose flour, for dusting

Neutral cooking oil (avocado or canola), if using parchment paper

½ cup baking soda

Pretzel or flaky salt, for sprinkling

Make the pimiento cheese: Mix the cream cheese, cheddar, mayonnaise, and red peppers in the bowl of a stand mixer with the paddle attachment on medium speed until combined, about 1 minute. Transfer to a container, cover, and refrigerate for at least 1 hour, or up to 2 weeks. Spoon into a serving bowl.

Make the pretzels: Cut the dough into eight equal portions and shape each into a ball. Arrange on a lightly floured work surface, dust with flour, and cover with a kitchen towel. Let stand for 15 minutes.

Line two large baking sheets with parchment paper or silicone mats. If using parchment, brush the paper with oil. On an unfloured work surface, roll and stretch one piece of dough under your palms into a 22-inch rope, moving your hands from the center toward the two ends as you roll. To shape the pretzel, curve the rope into an upside-down U shape, with the ends facing you. About one-third from the bottom, cross and twist the rope ends once. Fold down the curved top, stopping about an inch from the rope ends so it looks like a pretzel. Transfer to a prepared pan. Repeat with the remaining dough, allowing four pretzels per pan. Cover each pan with a kitchen towel and let stand at room temperature for about 15 minutes while preparing the baking soda bath.

Position the oven racks in the top third and center of the oven and preheat to 400ºF. Bring 2 quarts water to a full boil in a large saucepan over high heat. Gradually stir in the baking soda, taking care the water doesn't foam over. Reduce the heat to medium for a steady but not rapid boil. Add one formed pretzel to the water and boil until it sets, about 15 seconds. Using a wire spider or pancake turner, remove the pretzel from the water and return to the baking sheet. Repeat with the remaining pretzels.

Sprinkle the wet pretzels with the pretzel salt. Bake the pretzels, switching the positions of the pans halfway through baking, until golden brown, 12 to 15 minutes. Transfer the pretzels to a wire cooling rack to cool.

Serve warm or at room temperature with the cheese.

TAKEAWAYS

- The baking soda bath gives pretzels their shiny glaze. Don't skip it.
- Look for pretzel salt at bakery suppliers and online. Or use flaky salt, such as Maldon.
- For store-bought pickled peppers, try my favorite brand, Mama Lil's. Made in the Northwest, these peppers come hot or mildly spicy, so check the label for your level.
- Skip pre-shredded cheese because it doesn't break up well when beaten. Shred your own with a box grater, or cheat with the shredding disk on a food processor.
- The pretzels are best the day they're made, but you can freeze leftovers in a resealable plastic bag for up to 2 months. Reheat from frozen in a 350ºF oven for 10 minutes.

Carrot Hummus with Crudités

Pink hummus is my shit, but beets have a funk that not everybody loves. So carrots are the hero here, bringing sweet and earthy flavor and bright color that garbanzo beans are begging for. Use carrots with the deepest orange color you can find (they'll probably be local and organic). This beautiful golden hummus wants all the vegetables—more carrots, radishes, cucumber. Or go with your favorite flatbread crackers or warm strips of pita bread.

Serves 8 to 10; makes about 3 cups hummus

2 to 3 large carrots (about 11 ounces), scrubbed (but not peeled) and cut in half crosswise

4 large cloves garlic, crushed and peeled

2 sprigs fresh thyme

Kosher salt

¼ teaspoon black peppercorns

½ cup extra virgin olive oil, plus more for drizzling

1 (15.5-oz) can garbanzo beans (chickpeas), drained, liquid (aquafaba) reserved

⅓ cup tahini

3 tablespoons fresh lemon juice, plus more as needed

1 teaspoon Aleppo pepper, plus more for garnish

Raw vegetables, flatbread crackers, or pita strips, for serving

Put the carrots in a medium saucepan and add 2 cups water, 2 of the garlic cloves, the thyme, 1 teaspoon salt, and the peppercorns, adding additional water if needed to barely cover the carrots. Bring to a simmer over medium-high heat. Cover with the lid ajar and reduce the heat to medium-low. Cook at a brisk simmer until the carrots are tender, about 20 minutes. Drain the carrots, discard the peppercorns and thyme, and let cool completely.

While the carrots are cooling, make the garlic oil: Heat the oil and remaining 2 garlic cloves in a small saucepan over medium heat until small bubbles form around the garlic, 1 to 2 minutes. Remove from the heat and let stand to infuse until cool, about 20 minutes.

Combine the carrots, garlic oil with its garlic, garbanzo beans, tahini, lemon juice, Aleppo pepper, and 1 teaspoon salt in a food processor and process until smooth, about 1 minute. With the machine running, add 3 tablespoons of the reserved aquafaba and run to whip the hummus, about 1 minute more. Season with salt and more lemon juice, if desired. (The hummus can be refrigerated in a covered container for up to 1 week.)

To serve, transfer the hummus to a shallow serving bowl. Drizzle with additional olive oil, sprinkle with Aleppo pepper, and serve with the vegetables or flatbread crackers or pita for dipping.

TAKEAWAY

- If pink hummus is also your shit, substitute beets for the carrots. They're a little less sweet and a little more earthy, and the color really hits. Small beets work best. Scrub them well before cooking, but no need to peel—beet skins are edible.

Queso Flameado

Anytime I can scoop up melty cheese with a warm tortilla, I'm happy. When I was a kid, we'd walk across the border to this Mexican place called Bigo's, and every single time I'd get *queso flameado*—you probably know it as *queso fundido*, meaning "melted cheese"—which came out sizzling on a clay plate. As a grown-up, I've been borrowing a trick from Greek restaurants and igniting my fave dip with tequila. You don't need to flame it, but you should.

Serves 4 to 6

1 poblano chile

1 pound Oaxaca or mozzarella cheese, shredded

8 ounces Homemade Chorizo (page 225), or use store-bought fresh chorizo, casings removed if necessary

⅓ cup blanco tequila (optional)

Flour tortillas, warmed (see Takeaways), for serving

Position the broiler about 6 inches from the source of heat and preheat on high.

Put the chile on a broiler pan. Broil the chile, turning occasionally, until blackened and blistered on all sides, about 10 minutes. Transfer to a heatproof bowl and cover with plastic wrap. Let stand and steam for 10 minutes. Remove and discard the skin, stem, and seeds and dice the flesh; set aside.

Spread the cheese in a layer on one side of a large flameproof skillet, preferably cast-iron. Break the chorizo into small pieces and spread it on the other side of the skillet. Broil, occasionally stirring just the chorizo, until the cheese is melted and browned and the chorizo is cooked through, 10 to 12 minutes (be sure the skillet isn't too close to the broiler flame or the cheese will melt before the chorizo is cooked).

If flaming the queso, warm the tequila in a small saucepan over medium heat and pour into a small glass. Bring the skillet (with its lid), tequila, diced poblano, warmed tortillas, and a long match to the table (don't forget a trivet for the skillet). Pour the tequila over the queso. Dim the lights. Use the long match to carefully ignite the booze. Let the flame burn down on its own or cover with the lid to cut off the oxygen and kill it.

Sprinkle with the diced poblano and serve hot, with a large serving spoon and the warm tortillas. Spoon the cheese, chorizo, and chile into the tortillas, roll up, and go.

TAKEAWAYS

- Warm the tortillas while the queso broils (after step 3), either in a dry skillet over medium heat or directly over a medium-low gas flame until pliable—15 to 20 seconds per side (if using corn tortillas, about 10 seconds is good). As you warm them, stack and wrap the tortillas in a clean kitchen towel to keep the heat in.

- Just heat the tequila until warm, no more. If it gets too hot on the stove, it could ignite.

- If you flame the cheese, don't use a clay *queso fundido* server because it could crack. A flameproof metal skillet is a must.

Queso Flameado

Marinated Shrimp Skewers with Ginger Cocktail Sauce

When I want to whip up an app or a simple dinner, shrimp skewers come together in no time. If you like shrimp cocktail, it's in the family, but the sauce is full of ginger. Ginger juice, to be exact. It's a good thing to know how to make, as the juice is sharper and more concentrated in flavor than the grated root and can be used in soups, desserts, pickles, cocktails—anywhere you want that zip without any grit. I also use it in the shrimp's marinade here, because I'm extra.

Serves 6

Ginger Cocktail Sauce

1 cup ketchup

3 tablespoons fresh ginger juice (see Takeaways)

2 teaspoons prepared horseradish

Marinade and Shrimp

Finely grated zest of 1 lime plus 2 tablespoons juice

2 tablespoons dark sesame oil

1 tablespoon soy sauce

2 teaspoons fresh ginger juice (see Takeaways)

1 teaspoon light brown sugar

1 scallion, white part only, finely chopped (save the green part for garnish)

2 cloves garlic, minced

½ teaspoon shichimi togarashi

30 large (22–25 count) shrimp (about 1¼ pounds), peeled and deveined

1 scallion green, thinly sliced, for garnish

6 (6-inch) bamboo skewers, soaked in warm water for 30 minutes, drained (see Takeaways if grilling)

Make the sauce: Whisk the ketchup, ginger juice, and horseradish in a small bowl. (The sauce can be covered and refrigerated for up to 3 days.)

Marinate the shrimp: Whisk the lime zest and juice, sesame oil, soy sauce, ginger juice, and brown sugar in a medium bowl to dissolve the sugar. Add the chopped white scallion, garlic, and shichimi togarashi and whisk again. Pour into a 1-gallon sealable plastic bag, add the shrimp, and toss to coat. Close the bag and refrigerate for 30 to 60 minutes, no longer.

Cook the shrimp: Heat a ridged grill pan on the stovetop over high heat until very hot (see Takeaways for outdoor grilling). Holding the shrimp to retain a "C" shape, thread five shrimp onto a bamboo skewer through their tops and bottoms. Grill until the shrimp turn opaque, about 1½ minutes per side.

Arrange the skewers on plates, sprinkle with the scallion tops, and serve hot, with the sauce for dipping.

TAKEAWAYS

- While you can buy ginger juice, it's super-easy to make your own. Start with fresh, plump ginger with tight skin. You don't even need to peel it. For every tablespoon of juice needed, shred about 2 inches of the ginger on the large holes of a box grater. Scoop it into your fist and squeeze hard over a small bowl to catch the juice. That's it.

- The shrimp can also be cooked on an outdoor grill. Soak the skewers in water for at least 30 minutes, then drain. Heat a gas grill on high or build a charcoal fire and let the coals burn until they're covered with white ash. While cooking, slip a piece of aluminum foil under the exposed skewer "handles" to protect them from the heat and possible burning.

- Ponzu Dip (page 74) is also a good dip for the shrimp.

- If you're doing a passed app, you may want one shrimp per skewer, so soak 30 skewers.

Cashew Tzatziki with Za'atar Chips

Good things can happen when you get creative with ingredients you have on hand. This take on tzatziki was about using up some extra cashews, as they blend into a vegan cream that can act like yogurt. While the tzatziki tastes good freshly made, letting it ferment for a day or two gives it that sour tang of true yogurt. I serve it with baked pita chips featuring za'atar, a Middle Eastern herb-and-spice blend with tart, toasty notes that play nice with the dip.

Serves 8 to 10; makes about 3 cups tzatziki

Tzatziki

2 cups raw cashews

1 seedless (English) cucumber

8 cloves garlic, peeled

Grated zest plus ⅓ cup juice of 2 lemons

¼ cup coarsely chopped fresh dill, plus more for garnish

2 teaspoons sumac, plus more for garnish

Kosher salt and freshly ground black pepper

Fresh mint leaves, for garnish

Pita Chips

½ cup extra virgin olive oil

3 tablespoons za'atar (see Takeaway)

4 pocket pita breads, each split and cut into sixths

Flaky salt, for sprinkling

Make the tzatziki: Put the cashews in a bowl, add hot tap water to cover, and let stand for 2 to 4 hours, the longer the better. (Or cover with cold water and refrigerate overnight.) Drain well.

Coarsely chop half of the cucumber and set aside. Shred the remaining cucumber on the large holes of a box grater. A handful at a time, squeeze the excess liquid out of the shredded cucumber, then set the shredded cucumber aside.

With the food processor running, drop the garlic through the feed tube to mince. Add 1¼ cups water, the drained cashews, chopped cucumber, lemon zest and lemon juice, dill, sumac, and 1 teaspoon salt and process until smooth, about 1 minute. Transfer to a nonreactive glass or stainless-steel bowl and stir in the reserved shredded cucumber. Season with salt and pepper. (The tzatziki can be refrigerated in a covered container for up to 1 week. To ferment the tzatziki, see below.)

Make the chips: Position racks in the top third and center of the oven and preheat to 350°F. Mix the oil and za'atar in a large bowl. Add the pita wedges and toss well to coat. Divide the pita between two large baking sheets and sprinkle with the flaky salt. Bake, rearranging the wedges occasionally and changing the position of the racks from top to bottom and front to back halfway through baking, until the chips are crisp and golden, 12 to 15 minutes. Let cool. (The chips can be stored in an airtight container at room temperature for 1 day.)

Transfer the tzatziki to a serving bowl, sprinkle with sumac, dill, and mint, and serve with the chips.

TAKEAWAY

- You can make your own za'atar by pulsing 1 tablespoon dried oregano, 2 teaspoons sumac, 2 teaspoons sesame seeds, 1 teaspoon dried marjoram (or more oregano), 1 teaspoon dried thyme, and ½ teaspoon Aleppo pepper or crushed hot red pepper in an electric spice or coffee grinder until coarsely ground. Makes about 3 tablespoons.
- To ferment the tzatziki, loosely cover the bowl with plastic wrap and let it stand in a warm place (about 80°F) until bubbles form on the surface, 24 to 48 hours. Cover tightly and refrigerate until ready to serve, up to 3 days.

Sweet and Spicy Walnuts

Walnuts are one of the healthiest nuts, so I feel okay about adding some sugar to this addictive snack. It brings the sweet, salt, and crunch thanks to a glaze that pops with Mexican spices. I sling these on a board with some charcuterie and soft cheese to serve with drinks, or make a big batch to bag up and share.

Serves 6 to 8

1 pound walnut halves

1 cup powdered sugar

Neutral cooking oil (avocado or canola), for deep-frying

1 tablespoon ground guajillo chile

1 teaspoon flaky salt

½ teaspoon freshly ground black pepper

⅛ teaspoon cayenne pepper

Bring a large saucepan of water to a boil over high heat. Add the walnuts and boil for 30 seconds. Drain in a colander. Still in the colander, sprinkle the powdered sugar over the wet walnuts and toss until the sugar dissolves into a thin syrup coating. Let the excess syrup drain in the sink, stirring occasionally, while heating the oil.

Add enough oil to a large saucepan to come 2 inches up the sides and heat over high heat until the oil reaches 350°F. In two or three batches, without crowding, carefully add the walnuts to the oil (they will foam up) and deep-fry until they develop a deeper shade of brown, about 2½ minutes. Using a wire spider or slotted spoon, transfer the nuts to a large baking sheet and let sit until cooled and no longer sticky, 5 to 10 minutes. (They must be cool enough that they don't stick to the paper towels in the next steps.)

Transfer the walnuts to paper towels, cover with additional paper towels, and pat to absorb excess oil. Pour the walnuts into a medium bowl. Mix the guajillo, salt, black pepper, and cayenne pepper in a small bowl. Tossing the walnuts, sprinkle the chile mixture over them until coated. Cool completely. (The walnuts can be stored in an airtight container at room temperature for up to 2 weeks.)

TAKEAWAY

- Use walnut halves, not halves and pieces, because the small pieces tend to burn during frying.

Chapter 2

Soups and Salads

STAUB

Pork Posole Verde

Soup is one of my signatures, mainly because of an Adam Driver meme that started maybe my best content series ever, "Good Soup." I love the idea of a meal that's contained by one bowl but can still take you so many places. Posole verde is a hearty favorite, with a tomatillo base and lots of chewy hominy (*posole*). You can use beef or chicken, though I'm a fan of the traditional pork. This makes a big batch, so freeze the extra for anytime you don't feel like cooking.

Serves 12

1½ pounds tomatillos, husked and rinsed to remove any sticky residue

3 poblano chiles, halved lengthwise and seeded

3 Anaheim chiles, halved lengthwise and seeded

1 jalapeño chile, halved lengthwise (remove the seeds for a milder posole)

1 serrano chile, halved lengthwise and seeded (optional, for a spicier posole)

1 medium yellow onion, cut into ½-inch-thick half-moons

5 cloves garlic, peeled

2 tablespoons extra virgin olive oil, lard, or bacon fat (see Takeaway)

Kosher salt

1 tablespoon rainbow or black peppercorns

1 tablespoon cumin seeds

1 tablespoon Mexican oregano

1 bay leaf

2 pounds boneless pork butt, with fat cap intact

1 quart plus 2 cups chicken stock, preferably homemade (page 222)

½ cup fresh cilantro stems (reserve the leaves for garnish)

2 tablespoons fresh lime juice, plus more to taste

2 (15.5-ounce) cans hominy, drained and rinsed

For Serving

Shredded green cabbage

Thinly sliced radish

Cubed avocado

Fresh cilantro leaves

Mexican crema or sour cream

Lime wedges

Preheat the oven to 500ºF. Place a large baking sheet in the oven to heat at the same time. Combine the tomatillos, poblano, Anaheim, and jalapeño chiles (and the serrano, if using), onion, and garlic in a large bowl. Add the oil and toss to coat. Season with 1 teaspoon salt.

Spread the tomatillo mixture on the hot baking sheet. Roast, stirring occasionally, until the vegetables are charred and the tomatillos are bursting, about 20 minutes. Remove from the oven and let cool while proceeding with the recipe.

Meanwhile, heat a small skillet over medium heat. Add the peppercorns and cumin and cook, stirring occasionally, until toasted and smoking, about 1 to 3 minutes. Immediately transfer to a plate to cool. Grind coarsely in an electric spice or coffee grinder. Add the oregano and bay leaf and process until the mixture is finely ground.

Heat a large Dutch oven over medium-high heat. Add the pork butt, fat cap down, and cook without turning until some of the fat renders out, about 5 minutes. Continue to cook, turning occasionally, until browned all over, 5 to 7 minutes longer.

Transfer the tomatillo mixture to a blender or food processor. Add the 2 cups stock to the baking sheet, loosen any caramelized goodies with a wooden spoon, and carefully pour into the blender. Add the ground spice mixture, cilantro stems, and lime juice and process until smooth. Taste and add more lime if desired. Pour over the pork in the Dutch oven. Stir in the remaining 1 quart stock to barely cover the pork, adding water if needed. Cover and simmer over medium-low heat until the pork is falling-apart tender, about 2 hours. Stir in the hominy and cook until heated through, about 5 minutes.

Using the side of a large metal serving spoon, break the pork in the Dutch oven into spoon-sized chunks. (Or cut them into pieces with kitchen scissors.) Season the soup with salt. Ladle into large soup bowls and serve with cabbage, radish, avocado, cilantro, crema, and lime wedges on the side to add as toppings.

TAKEAWAY

- Instead of coating the tomatillo mixture with olive oil, you could use rendered fat to give the posole an even richer, deeper flavor. I always have it on hand because I cook so much, and because I hate to waste anything—especially the insane depth of flavor you get from meat fats. The next time you make bacon or pork shoulder or pan-seared steaks, here's what to do: Let the fat cool slightly, then pour it through a fine-mesh strainer or cheesecloth into a clean glass jar, leaving behind any browned bits. Seal it up and it'll keep for 1 to 3 months in the fridge.

Roast Cauliflower, Snap Peas, and Strawberries with Tarragon Pesto

"Hey, did you hear about Tarra?" I'd ask, and someone on the crew would always bite. "She's gon," I'd say, so pleased with myself. Everyone hated that joke. They couldn't hate on this salad, though. It serves a good number of people with just one big head of cauliflower. Not boiled to death like in the old days, but roasted golden brown and showing off with a bright green pesto and crunchy accents of flash-cooked sugar snap peas and sweet strawberries.

Serves 6 to 8

1 large cauliflower (about 2 pounds), cut into florets

2 tablespoons plus ½ cup extra virgin olive oil

12 ounces sugar snap peas, stems and strings removed

½ cup packed baby spinach leaves

¼ cup packed tarragon leaves

¼ cup pistachios, toasted and cooled (see Takeaways)

2 tablespoons fresh lemon juice

Kosher salt and freshly ground black pepper

Pinch of sugar

2 cups hulled and halved strawberries

Balsamic vinegar, for drizzling

½ cup crumbled cotija or ricotta salata cheese

Preheat the oven to 400°F. Spread the cauliflower on a large baking sheet, drizzle with the 2 tablespoons oil, and toss. Roast, stirring occasionally, until the cauliflower is crisp-tender and browned around the edges, about 20 minutes. Let cool completely.

Meanwhile, place a bowl of ice water near the stove. Bring a small saucepan of salted water to a boil over high heat. Add the sugar snap peas and cook just until they turn a brighter shade of green, about 1 minute. Drain, rinse under cold running water, and add to the ice water. Let stand for 5 minutes. Drain and pat dry with paper towels.

To make the pesto, process the spinach, tarragon, and pistachios in a blender until finely chopped. Add the lemon juice, ½ teaspoon salt, ⅛ teaspoon pepper, and pinch of sugar. With the machine running, gradually pour in the remaining ½ cup olive oil.

Toss the cauliflower, sugar snap peas, and strawberries in a serving bowl. Season with salt and pepper and drizzle with balsamic vinegar. Sprinkle with the cotija cheese and serve at room temperature with the pesto on the side.

TAKEAWAYS

- To toast the pistachios, heat a medium skillet over medium heat. Add the pistachios and cook, stirring often, until fragrant and lightly browned, 4 to 5 minutes. Transfer to a plate to cool.
- You can also toast nuts in the oven, if you're into a hands-off method that's less likely to burn things if you get distracted. The even heat gives you consistent color and flavor, and it's especially good for toasting big quantities. Pistachios should bake at 350°F until they're fragrant and just golden, 6 to 8 minutes, with one good shake of the baking sheet halfway through.

Emerald City Chowder

Living in Seattle, I have a gripe with tourists lining up for New England clam chowder like it's a local specialty. Really experiencing a place means eating *that* place's food, and the Pacific Northwest is a seafood mecca in its own right. This chowder represents the Emerald City, with all the good shit I find fresh at Pike Place Market, plus fresh parsley juice that literally turns the soup green. Enjoy it with crusty bread or the Tender Biscuits on page 179.

Serves 8

8 ounces multicolored baby potatoes (about 8 potatoes), scrubbed but unpeeled

2 tablespoons extra virgin olive oil

1 small yellow onion, chopped

1 cup dry white wine

2 sprigs leafy celery tops

4 sprigs fresh thyme or ¼ teaspoon dried

3 dozen littleneck or cherrystone clams, scrubbed and soaked (see Takeaways)

⅔ cup diced pancetta

1 celery rib, diced

8 ounces sliced mushrooms, preferably maitake; or use king, oyster, chanterelle, or cremini (or a combination)

1 medium leek, white and pale green parts only, chopped (1 cup)

¼ cup unbleached all-purpose flour

2 cups heavy cream

1 cup coarsely chopped fresh parsley

Kosher salt and freshly ground black pepper

Goldfish-shaped crackers, for garnish

Finely chopped fresh chives, for garnish

Put the potatoes in a medium saucepan and add enough cold salted water to cover. Bring to a boil over high heat. Reduce the heat to medium and cook at a brisk simmer until the potatoes are tender when pierced with the tip of a small knife. Drain and rinse under cold running water. Let cool until easy to handle, then slice into thin rounds and set aside.

Meanwhile, heat 1 tablespoon of the oil in a large saucepan over medium-high heat. Add the onion and cook, stirring often, until softened, about 1½ minutes. Add the wine, celery tops, and thyme and bring to a boil. Add the clams, cover tightly, and cook, occasionally shaking the pot, until the clams have opened, 5 to 7 minutes. Using a slotted spoon, transfer the clams to a large bowl. Line a fine-mesh wire sieve with a moistened and wrung-out paper towel or cheesecloth, set over a large bowl, and pour in the cooking liquid to strain. Add water as needed to measure 1 quart cooking liquid and reserve.

Let the clams cool for about 5 minutes. Remove the clam meat from the shells and discard the shells. Coarsely chop the clam meat and transfer the clams and any juices to a small bowl.

Cook the pancetta with the remaining 1 tablespoon oil in a large saucepan over medium heat, stirring occasionally, until browned, about 8 minutes. Using a slotted spoon, transfer to paper towels to drain, leaving the fat in the pan. Stir the celery into the fat, cover, and cook over medium heat until softened, about 1 minute. Add the mushrooms and increase the heat to medium-high. Cook, stirring occasionally, until beginning to brown, about 5 minutes. Transfer half of the mushrooms to the bowl with the clams. Stir the leeks into the mushrooms remaining in the pan and cook until tender, about 2 minutes. Sprinkle in the flour and stir well. Whisk in the reserved clam cooking liquid and the cream, scraping up any browned bits. Bring to a boil, stirring occasionally. Using an immersion blender, puree the soup base in the pot.

Balled in a damp kitchen towel, wring the parsley over the soup for its juice. Add the reserved potatoes, clam meat and juices, the mushroom mixture, and half of the pancetta. Cook until steaming (not boiling), about 2 minutes. Season with salt and pepper. Ladle into bowls and top with crackers, chives, and pancetta.

TAKEAWAYS

- Mesh bags of small multicolored potatoes (white, red, and purple) are a common sight in the produce section. But you can use any kind of good-looking small potatoes, fingerlings to baby Yukon Golds.

- Clams should always be scrubbed and soaked before cooking to remove any grit. Scrub them under cold running water with a clean vegetable brush or dedicated clam brush, then put them in a large bowl. Add 2 tablespoons salt, fill the bowl with ice water, and stir to dissolve the salt as best you can. Let stand for about 1 hour. Drain and rinse well.

Summer Berry Panzanella

Seattle people appreciate summer in a very specific way, because it's as glorious as it is short. You learn to shovel in the stunning produce while you can, so this is a salad designed for lots of ripe berries (I ate handfuls in the restaurant walk-ins when it was blueberry time). While the classic dish depends on juice from tomatoes soaking into the bread, my take softens it with a simple vinaigrette, the bite of white balsamic punching up summer fruit. And grilling the sourdough gives you smoky, bitter hints that bring it all together.

Serves 4 to 6

3 tablespoons white balsamic vinegar

1 teaspoon Dijon mustard

¼ teaspoon kosher salt

⅛ teaspoon freshly ground black pepper

⅔ cup extra virgin olive oil, plus more for brushing

4 slices sourdough bread, cut ½-inch thick

3 ounces (about 3 cups) baby lettuce greens

3 cups assorted berries (such as raspberries, blueberries, and sliced strawberries)

1 ripe Hass avocado, pitted, peeled, and cut into bite-sized pieces

½ cup crumbled ricotta salata cheese

Combine the vinegar, mustard, salt, and pepper in a small bowl. Gradually whisk in the oil (or use an immersion blender).

Heat a ridged grill pan over high heat (or preheat a gas grill to high). Brush the bread on both sides with oil. Grill the sourdough, turning once, until toasted with grill marks, about 3 minutes total (or a little less on a grill). Tear the bread into pieces about 1 inch square. Let cool.

Toss the greens and bread in a large bowl with the vinaigrette. Add the berries and avocado and gently toss again to combine. Top with the cheese and serve immediately.

TAKEAWAY

- White balsamic vinegar gives you that sweet-tart flavor without the dark color that would stain the pale bread. White wine vinegar with a pinch of brown sugar can substitute.

Curried Butternut Squash Soup

Sometimes it's the small touches that make big flavor. At the heart of Indian cooking is the way whole spices are toasted to bring out their oils and aromas. And that's essential for the depth of the curry starring in this golden soup. If I haven't made the crispy croutons, I just serve it with warm naan for wiping the bowl.

Serves 8 to 10

1 teaspoon yellow mustard seeds

1 teaspoon rainbow or black peppercorns

2 green cardamom pods, seeds only

1 teaspoon crushed hot red pepper

1 teaspoon ground cinnamon

1 teaspoon ground turmeric

1 bay leaf, crumbled

2 tablespoons extra virgin olive oil

1 large yellow onion, chopped

2 cloves garlic, minced

1 tablespoon minced peeled fresh ginger

1 butternut squash (about 2½ pounds), peeled, seeded, and cut into 1½-inch chunks

1½ quarts Vegetable Stock (page 223)

1 teaspoon Maggi seasoning sauce or soy sauce

Kosher salt

1 cup coconut milk (not light), plus more for serving

Cilantro Chutney

2 cups packed cilantro leaves

3 tablespoons finely chopped red onion

1 teaspoon finely chopped fresh green chile (such as serrano)

1 clove garlic, minced

¼ teaspoon ground cumin

2 ice cubes

Extra virgin olive oil, as needed

Naan Croutons

1 pocket pita, split and cut into 1-inch squares

2 tablespoons extra virgin olive oil

Make the soup: Heat a small skillet over medium-high heat. Add the mustard seeds, peppercorns, and cardamom seeds and cook, stirring often, until they're lightly toasted and smoking, about 1 minute. Transfer to an electric spice or coffee grinder and let cool. Grind the toasted spices. Add the hot pepper, cinnamon, turmeric, and bay leaf and pulse to combine.

Heat the oil in a large Dutch oven or saucepan over medium-high heat. Add the yellow onion, garlic, and ginger and cook until softened, about 3 minutes. Add the spices and cook, stirring often, until fragrant, about 30 seconds.

Add the squash and stir well. Stir in the stock, Maggi, and 2 teaspoons salt. Cover and bring to a boil. Put the lid ajar, reduce the heat to low, and simmer until the squash is tender, about 20 minutes. Add the coconut milk and heat until hot but not boiling. Cool slightly. Puree the soup in batches in a blender (see Takeaways for tips on safe blending). (The soup can be cooled, transferred to a covered container, and refrigerated for up to 2 days.)

Make the chutney: Bring a half-filled medium saucepan of water to a boil over high heat. Add the cilantro and cook to set the color, about 30 seconds. Drain in a wire sieve and rinse under cold running water. Squeeze to remove excess liquid. Puree the cilantro, red onion, chile, garlic, cumin, and ice cubes in a blender. If the chutney seems too thick, with the machine running, thin it with olive oil, a teaspoon at a time. Transfer to a small bowl.

Make the croutons: Preheat the oven to 350ºF. Put the pita squares in a medium bowl, drizzle with the oil, and toss well to coat. Spread the pita squares on a large baking sheet. Bake, stirring occasionally, until crisp and golden, about 10 minutes. Let cool.

Reheat the soup over low heat until simmering. Ladle into bowls and top each with the croutons, a drizzle of chutney, and a teaspoon or so additional coconut milk. Serve hot with the remaining chutney on the side.

TAKEAWAYS

- I admit that blending hot food isn't the best kitchen practice. Steam kicks up in the blender and the contents splash out, even with the lid tightly closed. While the real solution is to wait, I don't. I swap the lid for a kitchen towel. Drape the towel (don't fold or double it) over the blender jar, hold it in place, and, starting on low speed, blend away. The steam escapes through the weave in the towel (use one you don't mind staining).
- This dish is vegan but can be made with dairy. Just substitute half-and-half or heavy cream for the coconut milk.
- This makes a large batch and freezes well for up to 3 months for another meal.
- For a simple lunch, you can use chopped cilantro or mint instead of the chutney, though it gives the dish a more flavorful finish and a beautiful color contrast. (The ice is what sets that wicked green.)

Blackberry and Quinoa Salad with Ginger Vinaigrette

I'm not a rabbit, and I'm not a fucking model. I'm hungry. So I like grains in salads, not just some sad lettuce or veg. This salad is the move if you want to make friends at the potluck. You can use different fruit or a mix, but choose fruits that are firm-ripe so they hold their shape. The salad is best soon after making it, but you can prep your quinoa and dressing the day before and assemble with the fruit just before go-time.

Serves 8

1 cup quinoa, preferably tricolor

½ teaspoon kosher salt

Dressing

⅔ cup neutral cooking oil (such as avocado or canola)

¼ cup unseasoned rice vinegar, plus more to taste

3 tablespoons finely chopped fresh ginger (no need to peel)

½ teaspoon shichimi togarashi, plus more to taste

½ teaspoon kosher salt, plus more to taste

2 tart apples (such as Granny Smith), cored and thinly sliced

1⅓ cups blackberries

½ cup crumbled feta cheese

Cook the quinoa: Put the quinoa in a fine-mesh sieve, rinse well under cold running water, and drain. (Don't skip this step, as it removes the bitter natural coating.) Transfer the quinoa to a medium saucepan and add 1¾ cups water and the salt. Bring to a boil over high heat. Cover tightly and reduce the heat to low. Simmer until the quinoa has absorbed the water, about 15 minutes. Remove from the heat and let stand, covered, for 5 to 10 minutes. Fluff the quinoa with a fork and transfer to a large bowl to let cool completely, stirring often. (The quinoa can be covered and refrigerated for up to 1 day.)

Make the dressing: Process the oil, rice vinegar, ginger, togarashi, and salt in a blender until smooth. (The dressing can be refrigerated in a covered container for up to 5 days.)

Gently toss the apples and berries with 2 to 3 tablespoons of the dressing. You should have about 4 cups cut-up fruit. (The fruit can be prepared, covered, and refrigerated for up to 12 hours.)

Toss the quinoa with the remaining dressing, and half of the fruit. (The salad can be covered and refrigerated for up to 6 hours.) Reseason the quinoa mixture with vinegar, togarashi, and salt. Top with the remaining fruit and sprinkle with the feta cheese. Serve chilled or at room temperature.

TAKEAWAYS

- Togarashi is a spicy and dry Japanese condiment. Shichimi togarashi is a "seven spice" version with seaweed, sesame and/or poppy seeds, ginger, sansho (Japanese pepper), and dried citrus peel (orange or yuzu). As a substitute, start with a spicy base of 1 tablespoon gochugaru (Korean chili flakes), Aleppo pepper, or pure ground guajillo, and mix in pinches of the ingredients mentioned above until you like how it tastes.
- In the summer, I sub in stone fruits (peaches, nectarines, plums, cherries) for the apples and berries. If using stone fruit, pit the fruit, leaving it unpeeled, and cut it into bite-sized pieces.

Cold Corn Soup with Tomato Salsa and Basil

When summer corn is in season and you can't think of enough ways to enjoy it, make this cold soup. It's refreshing as a light lunch or the start to a warm-weather dinner of grilled meat or fish. Just remember not to season it until it's fully chilled, because the temperature really affects what and how you taste. Salty-ass corn is no bueno.

Serves 6 to 8

Corn and Stock

6 ears corn, husked

1 large yellow onion, cut into quarters

4 sprigs fresh thyme

2 bay leaves

Kosher salt

Freshly ground white pepper

Salsa

10 multicolored cherry tomatoes, diced

1 tablespoon fresh lime juice

2 teaspoons seeded and minced jalapeño chile

1 teaspoon minced scallion

Kosher salt

To Serve

Sugar (optional)

Small or coarsely chopped basil leaves

Extra virgin olive oil

Cook the corn and stock: Combine the corn, onion, thyme, and bay leaves in a large saucepan and add enough cold water to barely cover. Bring to a boil over high heat. Reduce the heat to low and simmer until the corn is tender, about 10 minutes. With tongs, transfer the corn (but not the onion) from the cooking liquid to a colander and rinse under cold running water to cool. Remove the saucepan with the cooking liquid from the heat, but don't toss the liquid. You'll use it for the stock.

One at a time, stand a corn ear vertically on its wide end and use a large knife to cut the kernels from the cob. Transfer the kernels to a bowl. Holding one ear over the bowl, run the knife from the bottom to the top to scrape the corn "milk" from the cob into the bowl with the kernels. Repeat to scrape all the ears; you should have about 5 cups corn and its milk.

Chop the corn cobs in half and return to the cooking liquid. Bring to a simmer, reduce the heat to low, and simmer for 15 to 20 minutes. Using tongs, remove and discard the corn cobs, thyme, and bay leaves. Pour the corn stock with the onion into a bowl. You'll need about 4 cups stock; add water, if needed.

In batches, combine 4 cups of the corn kernels, 3 cups of the corn stock (including the onion), 1½ teaspoons salt, and ¼ teaspoon pepper in a blender. Blend until very smooth, about 1 minute (see Takeaways, page 59, for tips on safe blending). Transfer to a bowl and cool until tepid, about 1 hour. Cover tightly with plastic wrap and refrigerate until chilled, at least 4 hours or overnight. Adjust the thickness with the 1 cup remaining stock, as needed.

Make the salsa: Mix the remaining 1 cup of the corn kernels (and any additional kernels), cherry tomatoes, lime juice, jalapeño, and scallion in a small bowl. Season with salt. Cover and refrigerate for at least 1 hour, or up to 8 hours.

To serve, whisk the soup well, and season again with additional salt, pepper, and a pinch or two of sugar, if needed. Ladle the soup into wide bowls and scatter a ring of the salsa around the outside edge. Sprinkle basil over the salsa, followed by a drizzle of the oil. Serve immediately.

TAKEAWAYS

- To contain the kernels when cutting from the cob, you can stand the cob in a shallow baking dish—any size will do. The kernels will fall into the dish and not all over the counter.
- The soup should be well chilled before serving, so make it a few hours or even a day ahead.

Cantaloupe Gazpacho

I love melon season. I try to eat melons all the time during the Seattle summer, so I end up buying a lot and letting some get too ripe. This is the soup to make in that scenario. With a pretty garnish of chili flakes and fresh jalapeño, it's a choose-your-own-adventure of spice, and flavor is layered in every bite. It doesn't even need cooking—just be sure to serve the gazpacho ice-cold. In fact, you might want to pop it in the freezer for an hour or so to give it a deep chill.

Serves 6

1 large ripe cantaloupe (about 3 pounds)

½ medium yellow onion, coarsely chopped

½ cup packed cilantro leaves, including thin stems

¼ cup extra virgin olive oil

1 jalapeño chile, seeded and coarsely chopped

1 serrano chile, seeded and coarsely chopped (optional)

3 tablespoons fresh lime juice

1 tablespoon ground guajillo chile

1 teaspoon kosher salt

Garnishes

¼ cup thinly sliced cilantro leaves

1 teaspoon gochugaru (Korean chili flakes) or additional ground guajillo chile

1 jalapeño chile, cut into thin rounds

Extra virgin olive oil

Prepare the cantaloupe: Peel and seed the melon. Cut enough cantaloupe into a small dice to measure about 2 cups; transfer the diced cantaloupe to a bowl, cover, and refrigerate until ready to use for garnish. Cut the remaining cantaloupe into 1-inch chunks. You want about 6 cups chunked cantaloupe.

Make the gazpacho: Process the cantaloupe chunks, onion, whole cilantro leaves, oil, chopped jalapeño, serrano (if using), lime juice, guajillo, and salt in a heavy-duty blender or food processor. Transfer to a covered container and refrigerate until chilled, at least 2 hours, or up to overnight.

Garnish and serve: Combine the reserved diced cantaloupe, the sliced cilantro, and Korean chile in a small bowl. (The mixture can be covered and refrigerated for up to 4 hours.) Ladle the soup into six chilled soup bowls. Divide the cantaloupe garnish among the soups. Top with a few jalapeño rounds, drizzle with oil, and serve immediately.

TAKEAWAYS

- I like my gazpacho spicy, so I use both jalapeño and serrano chiles. You may want to use only one. If you're not sure, taste the chilled gazpacho, and if you want it spicier, puree the second chile with 1 cup of the gazpacho in a blender, then stir it into the remaining soup.
- If you aren't a cilantro fan, substitute basil or mint.
- When you pick a melon for this gazpacho, go for one that's even larger than 3 pounds if you can't find just the right size. Because leftover cantaloupe for fruit salads and snacking is always a good thing.

Tequila
2 Ounces
Pomegranate
Juice
½ Ounce
Lime Juice
½ Ounce
Simple Syrup
Shake & Strain
into Glass with Ice
Garnish with
Orange Slice

Warm Lacinato Kale Caesar with Crispy Chickpeas

Not all kale is tough as shit. The lacinato variety is way softer, almost like Romaine, with gorgeous leaves that taste slightly nutty and sweet. I want them to keep their structure and crunch, so instead of wilting the kale ribbons on the stovetop, I warm the dressing. Tossing with warm Caesar relaxes the greens for a nicer bite and helps the flavors of anchovy, egg yolk, lemon, and garlic soak in.

Serves 4 to 6

Crispy Chickpeas

1 (15.5-ounce) can chickpeas (garbanzo beans), drained and rinsed

2 tablespoons extra virgin olive oil

Flaky salt

Caesar Dressing

2 cloves garlic, peeled

4 anchovy fillets in oil, drained

1 large egg yolk

Finely grated zest of 1 lemon plus 2 tablespoons juice

1 teaspoon Dijon mustard

¼ teaspoon kosher salt

⅛ teaspoon freshly ground black pepper

¼ cup plus 2 tablespoons extra virgin olive oil

¼ cup plus 2 tablespoons neutral cooking oil (such as avocado or canola)

¼ cup freshly grated Parmigiano-Reggiano cheese

Kale

2 (6-ounce) bunches lacinato (dinosaur) kale, rinsed but not dried

Freshly grated Parmigiano-Reggiano cheese, for serving

Make the chickpeas: Preheat the oven to 425ºF. Line a large baking sheet with parchment paper. Pat the drained chickpeas completely dry with paper towels, then spread on the prepared pan, drizzle with the olive oil, and toss to coat. Bake, stirring occasionally, until lightly browned and crisp, about 20 minutes. Season with flaky salt and let cool completely.

Make the dressing: With the food processor or blender running, drop the garlic through the feed tube to mince. Add the anchovy fillets, yolk, lemon zest and juice, mustard, salt, and pepper and pulse to combine. Combine the olive oil and neutral oil in a liquid measuring cup. With the machine running, slowly pour the combined oil through the feed tube to thicken the dressing. Add the Parmigiano and pulse until combined.

Warm the dressing and toss the kale: Stack the kale leaves and cut crosswise, including the stems, into thin shreds. Transfer the dressing to a small saucepan and warm over low heat until just warm to the touch (do not let it simmer). Put the kale in a large metal bowl and pour the warm dressing over it. Toss with tongs until evenly coated and slightly softened, 1 to 2 minutes. Let stand for 5 minutes to allow the stems to tenderize.

Transfer the kale to a serving platter. Sprinkle with the Parmigiano and the chickpeas and serve. (The remaining chickpeas and salad dressing can be covered and refrigerated for up to 2 days.)

TAKEAWAYS

- Whenever you use kale, rinse it well to remove any grit hiding in the many, many crevices.
- If you don't enjoy your greens al dente, you can wilt the kale before dressing it. Heat 1 tablespoon olive oil in a very large skillet over medium-high heat. In batches (about one-third at a time), add the kale and cook, stirring often, until the ribbons soften to your liking (it should only take a few minutes, as you don't want the greens to get mushy). Transfer to a large bowl, add as much of the dressing as you like, and toss. Transfer to a serving platter and finish with the chickpeas and grated cheese.

Chapter 3

Mains

Crispy Salmon with Toasted Miso Corn

I've got the reps on salmon, partly because I live in Seattle, and partly because I spent plenty of time on the sauté line. So I know how to achieve crispy skin that releases from the pan without any awkward spatula action. The result is luscious fish capped with "sea bacon," which I love with sweet and deeply savory miso corn. While you can use frozen corn (and toasting is a good way to give it more flavor), go for the fresh ears in season when you can.

Serves 4

Miso Corn

3 cups fresh corn kernels (from about 5 large ears), or thawed frozen kernels

2 teaspoons extra virgin olive oil

2 tablespoons unsalted butter

3 scallions, white and green parts, thinly sliced

1 cup cherry tomatoes

2 tablespoons white (shiro) miso

2 tablespoons hot water

2 teaspoons finely chopped fresh thyme

½ teaspoon freshly ground black pepper

Salmon

4 (6-ounce) skin-on salmon fillets, patted dry

Extra virgin olive oil

1½ teaspoons kosher salt

½ teaspoon freshly ground black pepper

1 scallion, cut into thin rings, for garnish

Lime wedges, for serving

Cook the corn: Preheat the oven to 200°F. Heat a large, heavy skillet (preferably cast-iron) over high heat until very hot. Toss the corn with the oil in a medium bowl, then add to the skillet and cook, without stirring, until the corn is beginning to brown, about 2 minutes. Stir and cook, without stirring again, until the corn is visibly browned on the edges, about 2 minutes more. Stir in the butter and scallions and cook until the butter melts. Stir in the tomatoes and cook until they are heated through, about 1 minute. Dissolve the miso in the hot water in a small bowl. Pour over the corn, stir to coat, then stir in the thyme and pepper. Transfer to a heatproof bowl and keep warm in the oven.

Cook the salmon: Wipe out the skillet with paper towels and return it to medium-high heat. Drizzle and rub the oil over the salmon and season with the salt and pepper. Place the salmon, skin-side down, in the skillet and lightly weigh down the fillets with a flat lid or plate that fits inside of the skillet. Cook, without moving the salmon, until the undersides are crisp and browned, about 3 minutes (see Takeaways for tips on knowing when it's ready to flip). Flip the salmon and remove the pan from the heat. Let stand for 1 minute to cook from the residual heat for medium-rare salmon, or longer if you prefer.

Transfer each fillet to a dinner plate and add the miso corn on the side. Sprinkle with scallions and serve hot with the lime wedges.

TAKEAWAYS

- Light pressure on the salmon is one secret to crisp skin. Any flat lid or plate wide enough to fit inside the skillet will do the trick. You're not squashing the salmon, just putting a little extra weight on top to increase contact with the hot skillet.
- Another secret is that you need to touch the flesh side of the salmon to know when it's got a good crust and is ready to flip. As the salmon skin cooks, excess liquid forms bubbles that eventually burst and allow the fish oils to crisp the skin. So, toward the end of the initial browning period, rest your fingers on the flesh, and if you don't feel any bubbling movement coming up from the underside, the salmon will naturally release from the pan without you having to force it.
- Miso is a Japanese fermented soybean paste that has gone mainstream. It comes in different strengths/colors. *Shiro* (white) is the most versatile, though it's actually pale yellow or beige. *Aka* (red) miso is darker and stronger in flavor. All miso is salty, so be careful when seasoning. In this dish, I don't add any additional salt to the corn mixture at all.

Furikake-Crusted Ahi Tuna Chirashi with Ponzu Dip

We all have our condiments of choice. Of necessity. Where you might carry hot sauce in your purse (respect), I have to have furikake on my countertop. If you love Japanese food, then you know the seaweed-based seasoning. There are tons of blends you can buy, but the homemade route lets you customize. Mine is heavy on mushroom and fennel seeds, and it's good on everything. Here it's a fast coating for seared tuna steaks served on sushi rice, with raw vegetables for color and crunch and ponzu to brighten.

Serves 4

Fennel Furikake

3 dried shiitake mushrooms, stemmed and coarsely chopped

1 sheet nori seaweed, coarsely chopped

2 teaspoons fennel seeds

2 teaspoons white sesame seeds

2 teaspoons black sesame seeds (or use more white sesame seeds)

1 teaspoon coarse gochugaru (Korean chili flakes)

Sushi Rice

1½ cups short-grain rice (or use long-grain rice)

¼ cup unseasoned rice vinegar

4 teaspoons granulated sugar

1 teaspoon kosher salt

Ponzu Dip

Finely grated zest of 1 lime

½ cup fresh lime juice

½ cup soy sauce

2 tablespoons mirin

4 (7-ounce) tuna steaks, cut about 1-inch thick

Neutral cooking oil (such as avocado or canola), for brushing

2 Persian cucumbers, diced

1 cup shelled edamame

½ carrot, cut into thin shreds (julienne)

Make the furikake: Pulse the mushrooms in a spice or coffee grinder until very finely minced. You should have 2 tablespoons. Transfer to a bowl. Add the nori to the spice grinder and pulse a few times until finely minced, but not a powder. You should have 2 tablespoons. Add to the bowl. Pulse the fennel seeds in the spice grinder until coarsely ground and add to the bowl. Add the white sesame seeds, black sesame seeds, and Korean chili to the bowl and mix well. (Makes about 6 tablespoons. The furikake can be stored in a covered container in a cool, dark place for up to 3 months.)

Cook the rice: Bring the rice and 3 cups water to a boil in a medium saucepan over high heat. Cover tightly and reduce the heat to low. Simmer until the rice has absorbed the water, about 20 minutes. Set aside, tightly covered, for 5 to 10 minutes.

Meanwhile, in a small saucepan over medium heat (or in a microwave oven in a small bowl on high), bring the vinegar, sugar, and salt to a simmer, stirring to dissolve the sugar. Set the rice vinegar seasoning aside to cool.

Make the ponzu dip: Whisk the lime zest, lime juice, soy sauce, and mirin in a small bowl. Divide among four small bowls for dipping.

Cook the tuna: Heat a large skillet (preferably cast-iron) over medium-high heat. Brush the tuna with oil, then sprinkle about 1 tablespoon furikake over each tuna steak and press gently to adhere. Add to the skillet and cook until the undersides are seared, about 2 minutes. Flip the tuna and cook to sear the other sides, about 2 minutes more. Transfer to a cutting board. Cut each steak across the grain (see Takeaways) into ½-inch slices.

To serve: Uncover the rice, sprinkle with the rice vinegar seasoning, and mix well with a wooden spoon. Mix the cucumber, edamame, and carrot in a small bowl. Divide the rice among four dinner plates. Add a tuna steak to each, fanning out the slices, then a portion of the cucumber mixture. Serve immediately, with the ponzu for dipping.

TAKEAWAYS

- In the furikake, feel free to substitute dried mushroom powder for the home-ground shiitakes.
- A mandoline or V-slicer does the best job when julienning the carrot.
- When cooking rice on the stovetop, remember that it will triple in volume, so choose a saucepan large enough to prevent boiling over.
- If you have a rice cooker, you can absolutely use it here. Follow the instructions for cooking 1½ cups raw rice.
- For the best-looking slices of tuna, cut across the grain (think about the lines in a plank of wood). Place the fish so the grain is running horizontally. Using a sharp, thin knife, cut perpendicular to the grain into ½-inch slices.

Spatchcocked Roast Chicken with Hasselback Potatoes

Roast chicken with potatoes is Hall of Fame comfort food, but there are tricks to making it memorable. First, I give the chicken a quick salt cure, as it's way more efficient than a sloppy brine. Spatchcocking—basically cutting the chicken down both sides of the backbone so you can spread the bird open—exposes more of the delicious skin to the oven heat, and it roasts faster than a whole bird. For the crispiest skin, I brown it on the stove in a skillet, then finish cooking with a second pan directly on top to hold potatoes for roasting them together.

Serves 4

1 (3½-pound) chicken

¼ cup plus ½ teaspoon kosher salt

1 tablespoon maple sugar or light brown sugar

2 tablespoons finely chopped rosemary or thyme leaves, or a combination

2 tablespoons extra virgin olive oil

6 small Yukon Gold or red-skinned potatoes (about 18 ounces total), scrubbed but unpeeled

¾ teaspoon freshly ground black pepper

2 cloves garlic, crushed under a knife and peeled

2 sprigs fresh thyme or rosemary

Spatchcock the chicken: Turn the chicken on its front (breast). Use kitchen scissors or a heavy knife to cut down both sides of the chicken backbone (the rib bones that connect there are on the thin side). Remove the backbone and reserve it for another use (such as stock, page 222). Place the chicken, breast side up, on the work surface and press hard on the breast to crack the breastbone so the chicken lies flatter.

Cure the chicken: Combine the ¼ cup salt, maple sugar, and 1 tablespoon of the rosemary in a small bowl and rub together with your fingertips to release the rosemary oils. On a baking sheet, generously sprinkle the cure all over the chicken and rub it in. Put the chicken on a wire rack and place over a large baking sheet or on a plate, rubbing in any of the salt cure that fell off. Let stand at room temperature to drain for 20 minutes to 1 hour. (Or refrigerate, uncovered, for up to 10 hours.) Discard the liquid in the pan. Rinse the chicken under cold water and pat completely dry with paper towels. Season all over with ½ teaspoon of the pepper.

While the chicken is curing, position a rack in the center of the oven and preheat to 425°F. (Allow at least 20 minutes for preheating, depending on your oven.) Heat 1 tablespoon of the oil in a large, heavy ovenproof skillet (preferably cast-iron) over medium-high heat, until hot but not smoking. Add the chicken, skin side down. Cook to start browning for 5 minutes without disturbing the chicken—do *not* try to move the chicken at this point, as the skin could stick to the pan.

(recipe continues)

TAKEAWAYS

- Look for smaller chickens (around 3½ pounds) at specialty markets, although some supermarkets may carry them. The overgrown supermarket variety is not ideal for this method, but if you have no other option, increase the cooking time for the chicken and potatoes. Be careful not to use kosher chickens, as they've already been salted.
- Sugar, either maple or brown, is an important part of the cure. First, it mellows the salt. But also, cured chicken doesn't brown as readily as uncured, and the sugar helps brown the skin. Keep in mind that the cure is rinsed to remove most of the sugar that could make the skin burn during the skillet browning.
- Pay attention to the size of your potatoes. They shouldn't be bigger than a medium egg to cook at the same time as the chicken. If they do end up undercooked, cook them on high in a microwave until tender, 3 minutes or so.
- To be sure you don't cut all the way through the Hasselback potatoes, try this trick: Put two chopsticks parallel to each other, leaving space between them, and top with a potato. Now when you cut down vertically into the potato, the chopsticks will stop your knife from reaching the board. There are Hasselback cutting tools, but I'm not a fan of gadgets, especially ones that only have one use in the kitchen.

While the chicken is browning in the skillet, cut the potatoes: Using a thin sharp knife, cut each potato crosswise in thin slices about ⅛ inch apart, stopping ¼ inch from the bottom. Do not cut the potatoes all the way through, as you want an accordion effect. (Potatoes cut in this way are called Hasselback; see Takeaways for tips.) Keeping the potatoes intact, place in a small bowl, drizzle with the remaining 1 tablespoon oil, sprinkle with the remaining ½ teaspoon salt and remaining ¼ teaspoon pepper, and toss to coat. Add the garlic cloves. Transfer to a pie plate or smaller skillet that will fit directly on top of the chicken. (Place the pie plate with the potatoes on the chicken while it is on the stove to give it a test run for balance.)

Slip the thyme sprigs under the chicken and place the skillet with the chicken in the oven. Place the pan with the potatoes on top. Roast for 30 minutes. Using kitchen tongs, transfer the potatoes to the skillet with the chicken and pour their oil and garlic over the chicken and potatoes. Continue roasting until the potatoes are tender and an instant-read thermometer inserted in the thickest part of the breast reads 165°F, about 10 minutes more.

Flip the chicken over, breast side up. Using kitchen scissors or a large knife, cut the chicken into serving portions in the skillet. Sprinkle the remaining 1 tablespoon rosemary over the chicken and potatoes and serve immediately, with a large spoon to serve the pan juices.

Scallops with Garlic Mashed Potatoes, Swiss Chard, and Lemon Brown Butter

Because they cook so quickly, scallops are a great choice for a weeknight dinner. But here's the thing. If you don't get the pan ripping hot, they won't cook right. It's gotta be hard and fast if you want a deep sear/caramelization but also want the scallops to cook through, but not too much. The smooth mashed potatoes and wilted chard's crunchy stems are perfect counterpoints, and everything gets boosted by brown butter with a lemony snap. If you want to go simpler, swap out the mashed potatoes for a crusty baguette, steamed rice, or quinoa.

Serves 4

Garlic Mashed Potatoes

1¾ pounds Yukon Gold potatoes, peeled and cut into 1-inch chunks

6 cloves garlic, crushed and peeled

5 tablespoons unsalted butter

¼ cup whole milk

¼ cup sour cream, at room temperature

Kosher salt and freshly ground black pepper

Scallops

20 large sea scallops (about 1¼ pounds) with feet removed (see Takeaways), patted dry

Kosher salt and freshly ground black pepper

2 tablespoons neutral cooking oil (such as avocado or canola)

¾ cup (1½ sticks) unsalted butter, sliced

1 lemon half

Swiss Chard

12 ounces red or rainbow Swiss chard, well rinsed but not dried, with stems removed and leaves cut crosswise into thin slices and then on the diagonal into ¼-inch strips

2 tablespoons neutral oil (such as avocado or canola)

Kosher salt and freshly ground black pepper

1 lemon half

TAKEAWAYS

- Scallops often have a small side muscle attached, known as the "foot." You'll find it easily because it feels tougher and more fibrous than the rest of the scallop, and it will get even tougher if you cook it. To remove the feet, grip with your fingers and gently tug—they should pull right off.
- This is a great example of how high heat can make or break your cooking. You need a hot-as-fuck skillet to caramelize the scallops, but you don't want blackened butter. So adjust and watch closely as the sauce comes together.
- To serve family-style, spread the potatoes on a platter and top with the chard, followed by the scallops and the brown butter.

Make the potatoes: Put the potatoes and garlic in a medium saucepan and add enough salted water to cover. Bring to a boil over high heat, reduce to medium, and cook at a low boil until the potatoes are tender, 15 to 20 minutes. Meanwhile, in a small saucepan, melt the butter, add the milk, and heat until steaming. Cover and remove from the heat. When the potatoes are tender, drain well, return to the saucepan, and add the sour cream. Using an electric hand mixer, mix until smooth (or mash with a potato masher), adding as much of the warm milk mixture as you wish. Season with salt and black pepper. Cover tightly and keep warm over very low heat.

Cook the scallops: Lay the scallops on a paper towel and dab the tops to dry. Season the scallops with salt and black pepper. Heat a large, heavy skillet over high heat until very hot. Add the oil and heat until shimmering. Add the scallops, flat side down, to start the sear. Cook the scallops until the undersides are browned, 4 to 5 minutes. Flip the scallops and brown the other sides, about 1 minute more, then transfer to a plate. Reduce the heat to medium. Add the butter to the skillet and cook, stirring, until the milk solids are toasty brown but not burned, about 3 minutes. Remove the skillet from the heat and squeeze in the lemon juice. Return the scallops to the skillet and set aside.

Cook the chard: In another large skillet, heat the oil over medium-high heat. A handful at a time, add the chard leaves and stems and cook until all the chard has been added. Cook, stirring often, until the chard is just tender, 2 to 3 minutes. Season with salt and pepper, then squeeze in the juice from the lemon half.

To serve, divide the mashed potatoes among four dinner plates. Top each with a portion of the chard, followed by five scallops. Drizzle the lemon brown butter on top and serve immediately.

Butter-Basted Steak with Blackberry Chutney

I got big on social media because of my chopping, everything from watermelon and chocolate to ice and McNuggets. But followers have seen me do a few other things again and again, like baste steak in butter. It's an ASMR bomb of sizzling, dripping deliciousness that does a lot for your meat in real life. It helps you get an even crust, adds depth to an already rich situation, speeds up cooking, and creates a browned-butter sauce to drizzle over your plate. Against the punch of blackberry chutney in this dish, it's a fatty miracle.

Serves 2 to 4

Steaks

2 teaspoons kosher salt

1 teaspoon freshly ground black pepper

2 strip or shell steaks (about 12 ounces each), 1-inch thick

Blackberry Chutney

2 (6-ounce) containers fresh blackberries; or 2⅔ cups frozen blackberries

¼ cup unseasoned rice vinegar

¼ cup packed brown sugar

⅓ cup finely chopped shallots

1 small clove garlic, minced

1 teaspoon kosher salt

½ teaspoon dry mustard

¼ teaspoon freshly ground black pepper

¼ teaspoon ground cinnamon

¼ teaspoon crushed hot red pepper

¼ teaspoon ground allspice

6 tablespoons (¾ stick) unsalted butter, cut into tablespoons

2 sprigs fresh thyme

1 clove garlic, peeled

TAKEAWAYS

- Most skillets can only comfortably hold two strip steaks. For more servings, go with smaller cuts like filets mignons (3 to 4 will fit without crowding). You'll trade a little marbling in the strip steaks for a lot of buttery tenderness.
- To give a nice piece of beef a crusty, tasty exterior, I let the seasoned steak rest before cooking for at least 30 minutes so the salt draws a little moisture to the surface. During cooking, these juices will concentrate and brown from contact with the hot skillet and help build flavor.
- When cooking steaks, the thickness is more important than actual weight. Thin cooks faster and thick cooks slower. A steak with a thickness of 1 inch will take about 4 minutes per side for medium-rare. For different doneness, adjust your timing.
- For the most tender bites of steak, cut against the grain. You'll see it as faint lines of muscle fiber running through the meat. Turn the steak so those lines run side to side, then use a sharp knife to cut straight down (perpendicular to the grain) into slices.

Season the steaks: Sprinkle the salt and pepper all over the steaks. Transfer to a wire rack set in a large baking sheet and let stand at room temperature for at least 30 minutes or up to 1 hour.

Make the chutney: Bring the blackberries, vinegar, brown sugar, shallots, garlic, salt, dry mustard, black pepper, cinnamon, hot pepper, and allspice to a boil in a medium saucepan over medium-high heat, stirring occasionally. Reduce the heat to medium and cook at a brisk simmer, stirring occasionally, until the mixture has reduced by about half and the juices are syrupy, about 15 minutes. Remove from the heat. Using an immersion blender, process the blackberry mixture until smooth. Let cool completely.

Cook the steaks: Heat a large, heavy skillet (preferably cast-iron) over medium-high heat for 3 to 5 minutes. Holding one steak with kitchen tongs, rub the fatty edge all over the bottom of the skillet to grease it—this should only take 15 seconds or so. Add both steaks to the pan and lightly weigh them down with a flat pot lid or sandwich press. Cook until the undersides are well-browned, about 2 minutes. Flip the steaks, weigh down, and cook to brown the other sides, about 2 minutes more. Flip the steaks again. Immediately add the butter, thyme, and garlic and stir until the butter is melted and the milk solids are toasty brown (not blackened), about 1 minute. Because the pan will be very hot, watch carefully for burning and reduce the heat as needed. Once the butter is melted, reduce the heat to medium. Using a potholder, hold the skillet by the handle to tilt the pan so the butter pools. With a soup spoon, continuously baste the butter over the steak for 2 minutes. Flip the steaks and baste for 2 minutes more for medium-rare steak. Transfer the steaks to a carving board to rest for 2 to 3 minutes. Remove the skillet from the heat.

For two servings: Transfer each steak to a dinner plate and add a dollop of chutney then a spoonful of the butter from the skillet.

For four servings: Slice each steak across the grain (see Takeaways), into ½-inch slices before topping with the chutney and butter.

Grilled Korean Short Ribs

I'm lucky to know some gifted Korean cooks (and their moms, who hook me up with the legit kimchi, not to mention home cooking that could crush most restaurants). They have short ribs absolutely dialed, marinating with sugar that gives you beautiful caramelization. I like to serve these ribs with kimchi and rice for traditional vibes, but mac 'n' cheese (page 113) is also an excellent sidekick.

Serves 6

1 cup soy sauce

½ cup mirin

¼ cup toasted sesame oil

¼ cup maple sugar or packed light brown sugar

4 cloves garlic, minced

2 scallions, white and green parts, minced

1 tablespoon gochugaru (Korean chili flakes)

1 tablespoon shichimi togarashi

1 tablespoon sesame seeds (toasting optional, see Takeaways)

5 pounds cross-cut short ribs (flanken or Korean cut)

Cooked white rice, for serving

Kimchi, for serving

Whisk the soy sauce, mirin, sesame oil, sugar, garlic, scallions, Korean chili, togarashi, and sesame seeds in a medium bowl to dissolve the sugar. Put the short ribs in a large ceramic or glass baking dish, pour in the marinade, and turn to coat. Cover and let stand for at least 30 minutes; or cover and refrigerate, turning occasionally, for up to 1 day.

To grill: Preheat a gas grill to high (600°F); or light a charcoal grill and let the coals burn until they're covered with white ash. Scrub the grate clean. Remove the ribs from the marinade, shaking off excess, and place on the grill. Cover and cook over direct heat, turning once, until well-browned but still medium-rare when pierced with the tip of a small sharp knife, 7 to 8 minutes.

To cook on the stove: Preheat the oven to 200°F. Preheat a large heavy skillet (preferably cast-iron) over medium-high heat. Turn on the stove vent, as these will smoke. In batches without crowding, add the ribs to the skillet and cook, turning once, until well-browned, 7 to 8 minutes. (Wipe out the skillet with paper towels between batches and keep the ribs warm in the oven while cooking the remaining batches.)

Serve the ribs with white rice and kimchi.

TAKEAWAYS

- Be sure to get the right cut of short ribs. Korean-style short ribs are cross-cut into wide ribbons about ½-inch thick. For this recipe, don't get English cut (where the meat is left on a single bone) or boneless—the ribs won't cook the same.
- This is a very flavorful marinade, so you don't have to marinate the meat very long. That's convenient, but Korean cooks are soaking their ribs overnight no matter what because that is the traditional way. Longer is always better if you can make it work.
- To toast sesame seeds, heat a small empty skillet over medium-high heat. Add the sesame seeds and cook, stirring occasionally, until fragrant and toasted, about 1 minute. Immediately transfer to a plate to stop the cooking and let cool.

Umami Chili

We get what umami is without needing to understand the chemistry. It's yumminess. But more accurately, it's savoriness, found naturally in things like cheese and tomatoes. It's the reason we love MSG (which is also natural, by the way). So, I load up my chili with umami-rich ingredients like mushrooms, soy sauce, and Worcestershire, alongside lots of chiles. And I toast my spices to boost their power so they can sharpen all that big flavor.

Serves 8 to 10

2 pounds ground chuck (80 percent lean)

2 guajillo chiles, stemmed, split, ribbed, and seeded

2 pasilla chiles, stemmed, split, ribbed, and seeded

1 morita chile, stemmed, split, ribbed, and seeded

Hot water, for soaking the chiles

3 tablespoons mixed rainbow peppercorns or black peppercorns

1 tablespoon Sichuan peppercorns

1 tablespoon cumin seeds

1 tablespoon coriander seeds

1 quart Chicken Stock (page 222, or use canned)

½ teaspoon cayenne pepper, or more to taste

¼ cup beef tallow, lard, duck fat, or olive oil

1 large yellow onion, finely chopped

12 cloves garlic, crushed into a paste (see Takeaways, page 26, for tips on garlic paste)

12 ounces mushrooms (such as cremini or stemmed shiitakes), coarsely chopped

1 (28-ounce) can Italian plum tomatoes (preferably San Marzano), drained and coarsely chopped

2 tablespoons soy sauce

1 tablespoon Worcestershire sauce

Kosher salt

1 bay leaf

Spread the ground chuck on a large baking sheet and freeze until partially frozen, about 30 minutes.

Preheat the oven to 400ºF. Put the guajillo, pasilla, and morita chiles in a medium bowl and add enough hot water to cover. Cover and let stand until softened, about 20 minutes.

Meanwhile, spread the rainbow peppercorns, Sichuan peppercorns, cumin seeds, and coriander seeds on a small baking sheet. Roast, stirring occasionally, until they smell toasted and fragrant, about 5 minutes (they may smoke a little). Transfer to a plate and let cool. Transfer the spices to a blender and process until ground. Drain the chiles, discarding the liquid, and add to the blender. Pour in the stock and cayenne and process until smooth. Set the chile sauce aside.

Transfer the partially frozen beef to a food processor and pulse until very finely processed, almost a paste. Heat the beef tallow in a large Dutch oven over medium-high heat until hot but not smoking. Add the onion and garlic and cook, stirring often, until softened, about 3 minutes. Add the ground chuck and cook, stirring occasionally, until it begins to lose its raw look, about 5 minutes. Add the mushrooms and cook until softened, about 8 minutes. Stir in the reserved chile sauce, tomatoes, soy sauce, Worcestershire, 2 teaspoons kosher salt, and the bay leaf and bring to a boil. Reduce the heat to medium-low and simmer uncovered, stirring occasionally, until the liquid has reduced and the chili is thick, about 2 hours.

Remove and discard the bay leaf. Ladle the chili into bowls and serve hot.

TAKEAWAYS

- I like to control the texture of ground beef by chopping it even finer in a food processor, but I make sure to partially freeze the meat before processing so it's not too soft to chop. The more meat surface exposed to the seasonings, the more flavorful the chili.

- Toasting spices brings their oils to the surface and increases their impact. While you can toast spices in a skillet, I often do it in the oven for more even heat distribution.

- For an over-the-top twist, try the chili on Big Cinnamon Buns (page 212). It's a crazy-good combo of sweet and spicy. To serve, put a bun in a soup bowl and spoon a big ladle of chili on top. (And it's okay to use store-bought buns.)

- If you prefer chili without the sweet roll underneath, top it with shredded cheddar cheese, sour cream, and minced red onion and jalapeño.

Beef Enchiladas

Enchiladas are in my DNA, and my family has lots of different recipes. The gold standard, the one I make the most, is beef and cheese with Mexican rice on the side. The beef is simmered until it's ridiculously tender, and the sauce built from that cooking liquid outclasses any other.

Serves 4 to 6

2 tablespoons beef tallow or olive oil, or more as needed

1½ pounds boneless beef chuck, cut into 3 or 4 chunks

1½ teaspoons kosher salt

½ teaspoon freshly ground black pepper

2 medium yellow onions, chopped

5 cloves garlic, chopped

6 guajillo chiles, stemmed and seeded (not toasted or soaked)

3 tablespoons tomato paste

4 cups Chicken Stock (page 222, or use canned)

Nonstick cooking oil spray

12 fajita-sized corn tortillas

1 cup shredded Oaxaca cheese

1 tablespoon seeded and finely chopped serrano chile, for garnish

Braise the beef: Heat the tallow in a large Dutch oven over medium-high heat until hot but not smoking. Put the beef in a large bowl and season with the salt and pepper. In batches without crowding, add the beef to the pot and cook, turning occasionally, until browned, about 5 minutes (you may need to add and heat more tallow or olive oil between batches). Transfer the beef to a plate, leaving any fat in the pot.

Add the onions and garlic to the pot and cook, stirring occasionally, until the onions soften, about 3 minutes. Add the chiles and tomato paste and cook, stirring often, until the tomato paste is drier and seared, about 2 minutes. Stir in the stock. Return the beef to the Dutch oven and add more stock or water to barely cover, if needed. Bring to a boil and cover tightly. Reduce the heat to low and simmer until the beef is very tender, about 2 hours. Using a slotted spoon, transfer the beef to a large bowl. Let the beef and cooking liquid cool separately. Using two forks or your fingers, pull the beef into shreds.

Make the sauce: In batches if necessary, transfer the cooking liquid and its vegetables to a blender and process until smooth. The sauce should coat a wooden spoon like heavy cream. If it's too thin, return to the saucepan and boil over high heat, stirring often, until it thickens. You should have about 4½ cups sauce. Stir about ½ cup of the sauce into the shredded beef. Transfer the remaining sauce to a medium skillet and place over low heat to keep warm.

Bake the enchiladas: Position a rack in the top third of the oven and preheat to 350°F. Spread a few tablespoons of the sauce in the bottom of a 10x15-inch baking dish. Place the baking dish, shredded beef, tortillas, and a plate near the stove. Using kitchen tongs, one at a time dip a tortilla into the warm sauce and transfer to the plate. Put 2 to 3 tablespoons of the beef in the bottom third of the tortilla, roll it up, and place it, seam-side down, in the baking dish. Repeat with the remaining tortillas and beef, fitting the enchiladas snugly together. Spoon any remaining sauce over the beef. Stir any remaining beef into the remaining sauce and pour it over the enchiladas. Sprinkle the cheese on top. Bake until the cheese is melted and the sauce is bubbling, about 25 minutes. Sprinkle with the serrano chile and serve.

Yucatan Pulled Pork

Cochinita is pork slowly simmered in a red sauce of ground spices and orange juice. It's a recipe from the "stick it in the oven and forget about it" school of cooking. Served with rice and tart green salsa, it may be a simple meal, but it could not be tastier. Leftovers work in tacos, enchiladas, and tortas.

Serves 10 to 12

Pork

1 (3-inch) cinnamon stick, broken into shards

¼ cup/40 annatto seeds (see Takeaways)

1 tablespoon black peppercorns

2 whole cloves

1 tablespoon dried oregano (preferably Mexican, see Takeaways)

1 cup fresh orange juice

8 cloves garlic, peeled

2 teaspoons kosher salt

1 (3-pound) boneless pork butt or shoulder roast

1 medium yellow onion, cut into thick slices

2 limes, cut into halves

1 cup Chicken Stock (page 222, or use canned)

For Serving

Cooked white rice

Salsa Crema (see Chicken Chilaquiles Suizas, page 95)

Warm corn tortillas

Fresh cilantro leaves

Sliced lime

Rub the pork: Heat a medium skillet over medium heat. Add the cinnamon, annatto, peppercorns, and cloves and toast, stirring occasionally, until the spices smell fragrant and toasty, about 2 minutes. Immediately transfer to a plate and let cool. Add the oregano, then finely grind the mix in an electric spice or coffee grinder. Pour into a blender, add the orange juice, garlic, and salt and process until smooth. Pour into a large bowl, add the pork, and mix well to coat. Let stand at room temperature for 30 to 60 minutes.

Preheat the oven to 500°F. Place the pork on a wire rack set in a large baking sheet. Roast, turning occasionally, until nicely browned, about 20 minutes. Transfer the pork to a Dutch oven. Reduce the oven temperature to 325°F.

Add the onion and limes to the Dutch oven along with the stock. Cover tightly and bake until the pork is very tender, 2½ to 3 hours.

Transfer the roast to a chopping board. If the roast was tied, discard the twine. Using kitchen tongs, remove the limes, squeezing the juice from the hulls over the pork. Pull the pork into shreds with two forks, mixing in the onions from the pot. (Or put on kitchen-safe gloves to avoid staining your hands and pull the hot meat apart with your fingers.) Transfer the pork to a serving platter. Pour some of the cooking liquid into a serving bowl.

Spoon the pork over bowls of rice and drizzle with the cooking juices. Serve rice, salsa crema, tortillas, cilantro, and sliced lime on the side.

TAKEAWAYS

- Annatto (also called achiote), a brick-red seed that's used in Mexican cooking, is sold at Mexican markets and many supermarkets. It stains like hell, both kitchenware and clothes. You're kinda out of luck on the clothes, but you can scrub kitchenware with nonabrasive citric acid–based cleaners like Bar Keepers Friend.

- Mexican oregano has more stems and a funkier aroma than the familiar Mediterranean variety, and using it here will give authentic flavor.

Lamb Shanks with Orzo Pilaf

Lamb shanks are cheaper and pack more flavor than other cuts of lamb, and few meat cuts in general are more succulent after a braise. Then you have the toasted flavors of the cumin and orzo, the bright acid of yogurt and lemon juice, and the freshness of mint. Straight dope.

Serves 4

Lamb

4 lamb shanks (about 1 pound each)

Kosher salt and freshly ground black pepper

¼ cup unbleached all-purpose flour

2 tablespoons extra virgin olive oil

1 medium leek, white and pale green part only, chopped

1 medium carrot, chopped

1 medium celery stalk, chopped

4 cloves garlic, crushed and peeled

1 tablespoon tomato paste

1 tablespoon dried oregano

½ teaspoon Aleppo pepper or crushed hot red pepper

1 cup dry white wine

2 cups Chicken Stock (page 222, or use canned)

Burnt Cumin Yogurt

2 teaspoons cumin seeds

½ cup plain Greek yogurt (low-fat or whole-milk)

½ cup whole milk

2 teaspoons Aleppo pepper or 1 teaspoon crushed hot red pepper

Kosher salt

Orzo Pilaf

2 tablespoons unsalted butter

1 cup orzo

2 cups Chicken Stock (page 222, or use canned)

½ teaspoon kosher salt

Cook the lamb: Preheat the oven to 325ºF. In a large bowl, season the lamb with 1½ teaspoons salt and ½ teaspoon black pepper, then toss with the flour to coat. Heat the oil in a large Dutch oven over medium-high heat. In batches, add the lamb, shaking off the excess flour, and cook, turning occasionally, until browned, about 6 minutes. Transfer the shanks to a plate.

Add the leek, carrot, celery, and garlic to the Dutch oven and cook, stirring occasionally, until browned, about 5 minutes. Stir in the tomato paste and cook until seared, about 2 minutes. Add the oregano and Aleppo pepper and cook until fragrant, about 30 seconds. Add the wine and bring to a boil. Stir in the stock and return the lamb to the Dutch oven (the liquid doesn't have to cover the lamb). Bring to a boil and cover tightly. Transfer to the oven and bake, turning the lamb occasionally, until tender when pierced with a thin sharp knife, about 2 hours. Transfer the lamb to a plate and cover with aluminum foil to keep warm. Season the sauce with salt and pepper.

Make the cumin yogurt: Heat a small skillet over medium heat. Add the cumin seeds and cook, stirring occasionally, until they are deeply toasted and smoking, about 2 minutes. Transfer to a plate and let cool. Coarsely crush the seeds in a mortar with a pestle, in an electric spice grinder, or on a chopping board under a heavy saucepan. Mix the crushed cumin with the yogurt, milk, and Aleppo pepper in a small bowl and season with salt.

Make the orzo: Melt the butter in a medium saucepan over medium-high heat. Add the orzo and cook, stirring occasionally, until most of the orzo is toasted, about 2 minutes. Add the stock and salt and bring to a boil. Cover tightly and reduce the heat to medium-low. Cook at a brisk simmer until the orzo is tender and has absorbed the liquid, about 12 minutes. Uncover and cook, stirring often (don't let it stick!) to evaporate the remaining liquid, 1 to 2 minutes. Transfer the orzo to a deep serving platter.

Finish the lamb: In batches, if necessary, transfer the lamb cooking liquid and its vegetables to a blender and process until smooth and thickened. (See Takeaways, page 59, for tips on safe blending.) Arrange the lamb shanks over the orzo and nap with the sauce. (Nap, or *nappe*, is a French word that means to coat a piece of food with an even layer of sauce.) Serve the orzo and lamb with the yogurt on the side.

TAKEAWAYS

- For a quicker weeknight meal, you can easily adjust this recipe to use 4 lamb shoulder chops instead of shanks. Use about half of all the other ingredients, except the burnt cumin yogurt and the orzo, and make sure the leek, carrot, and celery are very finely chopped so they get tender at the same time as the lamb. Brown the chops in a large, deep skillet for about 5 minutes, then proceed as directed, but simmer on the stove over medium-low heat just until the chops are tender, about 20 minutes.
- The light coating of flour on the lamb will give body to the sauce.

Chicken Chilaquiles Suizas

My Aunt Jackie is famous in our family for her enchiladas Suizas, rolled with a creamy green sauce and filled with lots of cheese and chicken. I always looked forward to them as a kid, but after really learning to cook, I saw her method for what it was: a quick-and-dirty pleasure. Picture shredded store-bought rotisserie chicken rolled into tortillas with jarred green salsa and cooked in the microwave. Upgrading involved turning basic enchiladas into the skillet dinner known as chilaquiles. They're called Suizas (Swiss) because of all the dairy, including crema and cheese. Much love to my auntie, but the microwave took it too far.

Serves 6 to 8

Salsa Crema

3 cups Roasted Salsa Verde (page 230)

¾ cup Mexican crema or heavy cream

Chilaquiles

Nonstick cooking oil spray

18 corn tortillas, torn or cut into quarters

2 cups shredded cooked chicken (such as rotisserie chicken or the shredded chicken from Creamy Chicken Tortas, page 136)

3 cups shredded Oaxaca or mozzarella cheese

Toppings

Thinly sliced radishes

Diced ripe avocado

Cilantro leaves

Mexican crema or crème fraîche, in a squeeze bottle

Sliced lime

Make the salsa crema: Whisk or blend together the salsa and crema. If you want it very smooth, use a blender to combine.

Make the chilaquiles: Preheat the oven to 350ºF. Mist two large baking sheets with the cooking spray. Divide the tortilla wedges between the pans and mist the chips with the spray. Bake, stirring occasionally, until the tortillas are lightly toasted, about 15 minutes. Remove from the heat to cool and crisp. Transfer to a bowl and set aside. Leave the oven on.

Mist one of the baking sheets again with nonstick spray. Spread half of the tortillas on the pan and top with half of the salsa crema, all of the chicken, and half of the cheese. Cover with the remaining tortillas. Spread the remaining salsa crema on top and sprinkle with the remaining cheese. Bake until the salsa crema is bubbling and the cheese is melted, about 25 minutes.

Sprinkle with the radishes, avocado, and cilantro, squirt a zigzag of crema on top, and serve with the lime.

TAKEAWAY

- You can substitute store-bought tortilla chips for the baked ones. Unsalted are the best choice as they won't throw off the seasoning.

Lemon-Pepper Chicken Wings with Green Ranch Dip

It's a never-ending war for me when it comes to wings. Lemon pepper or classic Buffalo? Because their finishes are so easy, I often cook one batch of wings and serve both styles at the same meal (see the variation). I usually deep-fry the wings with a double-fry method that makes them especially crispy, but I've included an oven-roasted approach.

Serves 4 to 6

Lemon Pepper

Finely grated zest of 2 large lemons (use a Microplane), about ¼ loosely packed cup

1 tablespoon coarsely ground rainbow or black pepper

½ teaspoon kosher salt

½ teaspoon citric acid (also called sour salt), optional, for additional tartness

Wings

4 pounds chicken wings, chopped between the joints into three pieces (drumettes, flats, and wing tips), tips discarded or reserved for making stock (or buy precut "party wings")

2 tablespoons Diamond Crystal kosher salt (see Takeaways)

1 tablespoon granulated sugar

Neutral cooking oil (such as avocado or canola), if deep-frying the wings

To Serve

Lemon wedges, for squeezing

Green Ranch Dressing (page 235)

Make the lemon pepper: Preheat the oven to 170°F. Line a large baking sheet with parchment paper. Spread the lemon zest on the prepared pan and bake, stirring occasionally, until the zest is dry, about 35 minutes. Let cool completely. Combine the zest with the pepper, salt, and citric acid (if using).

Cure the wings: Put the wings in a large bowl. Whisk the salt and sugar in a small bowl and sprinkle over the wings, tossing for even distribution. Transfer the wings to a wire cooking rack set over a large baking sheet, cover, and let stand at room temperature for at least 20 minutes, or up to 1 hour (see Takeaways). Pat the wings dry with paper towels.

To deep-fry the wings, preheat the oven to 200°F. Pour enough oil into a large saucepan to come about 2 inches up the sides and heat over high heat to 325°F on a deep-frying thermometer. Set a wire cooling rack in a large baking sheet. In batches without crowding, deep-fry the wings until lightly golden, 8 to 10 minutes. They will not be cooked through at this point. Using a wire spider or slotted spoon, transfer the wings to the wire rack and let drain and cool for 10 minutes, or up to 1 hour.

Just before serving, reheat the oil to 375°F. In batches without crowding, deep-fry the par-cooked wings until GBD (Golden Brown Delicious), about 3 minutes. (Break open a wing to check for doneness—there should be no sign of pink at the joints. Return to the oil and fry longer, if needed.) Using the wire spider, return the wings to the wire rack. Keep warm in the oven until all the wings are fried.

Transfer the wings to a large bowl and sprinkle with the lemon pepper, tossing for even distribution. Serve hot, with the lemon wedges for squeezing and the ranch for dipping.

Buffalo Wings:

Omit the lemon pepper. Melt 6 tablespoons unsalted butter (¾ stick) in a small saucepan. Add 1 cup hot sauce (preferably Frank's) and whisk to combine. Pour into a large bowl. Add the cooked wings and toss to coat. Serve with the Cotija Dressing (page 233) as a dip.

TAKEAWAYS

- It's worth making a double batch of the lemon pepper for other uses. Stored in an airtight container in a cool, dark place, it will keep for about 1 month. Try it on everything from fish to corn on the cob.
- If you use Morton's kosher salt in the cure (saltier than Diamond Crystal), cut the amount to 1 tablespoon.
- I always cure chicken before cooking. The salt pulls moisture from the meat so the wings cook up extra-crispy, whether baked or fried. If I know I'm gonna be gone all day, I'll coat the wings in the morning and refrigerate them uncovered to cure while I'm away. Because the longer cure really delivers the goods.
- Drain the wings, as directed, on a wire rack. Do not be tempted to drain them on paper, like your grandma did. The sugar in the cure will glue them to the paper.
- To roast the wings, preheat the oven to 425°F. Line a large baking sheet with parchment paper. Spread the wings on the prepared pan and roast, flipping the wings over after 20 minutes. Continue roasting until the wings are browned and cooked through, about 25 minutes more.
- There is a better way to eat chicken wings, called the "meat umbrella" trick. I learned it from my buddy Matt Groark of Groark Boys BBQ. Grab a wing flat at one end and stand it upright on your plate. Push the meat down into a tasty lump, like sliding an umbrella on its rod. More in your mouth, not on your hands.

MOUNTAIN FRESH
Rainier

Stuffing-Crusted Turkey with Gravy and Cranberry Sauce

One spring day, I had a craving for Thanksgiving dinner. That pushed me to figure out a much quicker hack for all the flavors of a full-blown holiday feast. If I'm honest, this is mainly a way for me to eat stuffing. Serve it with roasted sweet potatoes and some green beans if you really want to get in the mood.

Serves 4

Gravy

2 tablespoons unsalted butter

¼ cup unbleached all-purpose flour

2 cups Turkey Stock or Chicken Stock (page 222, or canned)

½ teaspoon Maggi seasoning sauce or soy sauce

Kosher salt and freshly ground black pepper

Turkey

2 cups buttermilk

1 teaspoon onion powder

1 teaspoon celery seed

1 teaspoon dried marjoram

1 teaspoon kosher salt

¼ teaspoon freshly ground black pepper

1 pound turkey breast cutlets, cut into strips about 6 inches long and 2 inches wide

2 cups panko (Japanese breadcrumbs)

6 tablespoons (¾ stick) unsalted butter, melted

To Serve

1 tablespoon finely chopped fresh rosemary

1 tablespoon finely chopped fresh sage

1 tablespoon finely chopped fresh thyme

Cranberry Sauce with Orange, Maple, and Thyme (page 237)

Make the gravy: Melt the butter in a medium saucepan over medium heat. Sprinkle in the flour and whisk until smooth. Let bubble, whisking often, until pale brown, about 1½ minutes. Gradually whisk in the stock and Maggi sauce and bring to a simmer. Reduce the heat to medium-low and simmer, whisking occasionally, until lightly thickened, about 5 minutes. Season with salt and pepper. Remove from the heat and cover to keep warm.

Make the turkey: Whisk the buttermilk, onion powder, celery seed, marjoram, salt, and pepper in a medium bowl. Add the turkey strips and mix to coat. Cover and refrigerate for 15 to 30 minutes. Put the panko in another medium bowl.

Preheat the oven to 350°F. Brush a large baking sheet with some of the melted butter. A few strips at a time, remove the turkey from the buttermilk and shake off the excess. Add to the panko, toss to coat, and place on the prepared pan. Drizzle the turkey strips with the remaining butter. Bake for 15 minutes. Flip the turkey and bake until the strips are golden brown and cooked through, about 10 minutes more.

To serve: Mix together the rosemary, sage, and thyme. Transfer the turkey to a platter and sprinkle with the herbs. Reheat the gravy, if needed. Serve the turkey immediately with the gravy and cranberry sauce.

TAKEAWAY

- The Maggi in the gravy acts as a color enhancer more than a flavoring, although it will add a touch of umami. It's an old-school sauce that pops up in recipes across the world.

Chapter 4

Pasta, Pizza, and Rice

SPAM

Seafood Fideo

Other kids had SpaghettiOs. I had fideo—tomato broth with soft, skinny noodles. This grown-up version takes it to a place more like paella, with clams, chorizo, and potent spices that add complexity to the Mexican comfort classic. If you want it a little fancier, try it with mussels. If mollusks aren't your thing, I've got a method for shrimp. I want everybody to be happy, just like the fideo does.

Serves 4

24 littleneck clams, scrubbed and soaked (see Takeaways, page 55)

¼ cup extra virgin olive oil

1 link (2½ ounces) firm smoked Spanish chorizo, diced

1 yellow onion, finely chopped

3 cloves garlic, minced

1 (10-ounce) bag fideos, coarsely crushed

2 teaspoons chili powder

2 teaspoons whole cumin

2 teaspoons dried oregano, crumbled

2 teaspoons sweet paprika

1 (28-ounce) can Italian plum tomatoes in juice, undrained

1 (16-ounce) can tomato-clam juice (such as Clamato); or 1 cup tomato juice plus 1 cup clam juice; or 2 cups tomato juice

Kosher salt

Chopped fresh cilantro, for serving

Lime halves, for serving

Heat the oil and chorizo in a large heavy skillet over medium heat, stirring often, until the chorizo is browned, about 5 minutes. Add the onion and garlic and cook, stirring occasionally, until softened, about 3 minutes.

Add the fideos and cook, turning occasionally, until lightly toasted, about 2 minutes. Add the chili powder, cumin, oregano, and paprika and stir until fragrant, about 30 seconds. Stir in the tomatoes (with their juices) and the tomato-clam juice. Bring to a boil over high heat, coarsely breaking up the tomatoes with the side of a spoon. Add the clams and tightly cover the skillet.

Reduce the heat to medium-low and simmer, stirring occasionally, until the fideo is very tender and has absorbed most of the liquid and all the clams have opened, 5 to 7 minutes. Discard any unopened clams. Season with salt.

Spoon the clams and broth into serving bowls, sprinkle with the cilantro, and serve hot with the lime halves.

TAKEAWAYS

- You can substitute mussels for the clams. PEI (Prince Edward Island) mussels need minimal cleaning, as they don't have "beards" and don't need to be soaked. If you have standard mussels, use pliers to pull off the beards, then scrub and soak the mussels as you would clams. You can also use 1 pound medium (31-35 count) shrimp, peeled and deveined, but to avoid overcooking, don't add them until the fideos have cooked for 2 minutes. If the shrimp aren't opaque when the fideo is done, just let the covered skillet stand off the heat for a few minutes to finish the cooking. Don't worry about overcooking these noodles. They're supposed to be soft and comforting.
- Fideo is sold in coils at Mexican markets and in the international or pasta aisle of supermarkets. To sub in standard angel hair pasta, break the noodles in half (2-inch lengths) for 2 heaping cups.

French Gnocchi Carbonara

These fluffy pillows are my favorite "pasta"—crispy-on-the-outside nuggets drowned in sauce. This is the French way to make gnocchi, with flour instead of potatoes. Not gonna lie, it makes the recipe harder. In fact, my editor didn't want me to include it in the book because she was sure someone would struggle and come at me. But French gnocchi are lighter in texture, richer in flavor, and more consistent overall. So I'm trusting that you guys want to grow—and that you can find my gnocchi videos. I'm also trusting you to use metric weights for the dough (it won't turn out otherwise, so I'm not even giving you cup measurements). What do you get for putting in the work? Custardy gnocchi that get beautifully browned and finished with classic Italian carbonara. Extra cheese always.

Serves 4 to 6

French Gnocchi

170 g (1½ sticks) unsalted butter, cut into cubes

2.8 g kosher salt

310 g unbleached all-purpose flour

6 large eggs, at room temperature, beaten together until combined

Carbonara Sauce

4 ounces diced pancetta (about ⅔ cup)

3 tablespoons neutral cooking oil (such as avocado or canola)

1¼ packed cups freshly grated Parmigiano-Reggiano, plus more for serving

4 large egg yolks, at room temperature

Freshly ground black pepper

Make the gnocchi: Bring a large saucepan of salted water to a simmer over high heat, adjusting to maintain the simmer (don't boil). Place a bowl of cold water near the stove.

Meanwhile, in a medium saucepan, bring a scant 1½ cups water, the butter, and salt to a full boil over medium-high heat, stirring occasionally to completely melt the butter without letting the liquid reduce. Dump in the flour all at once and stir well to make a very soft dough. Reduce the heat to medium. Continue stirring until a film begins to form on the pan bottom, about 1 minute. Transfer to the bowl of a stand mixer and beat with the paddle attachment (or use a large bowl and hand mixer) on medium speed for about 30 seconds (long enough to cool slightly so the eggs don't curdle). Increase the speed to medium-high, gradually beat in the eggs, and continue mixing to make a cohesive, sticky dough, about 30 seconds more.

Using a silicone spatula, scrape the dough into a large disposable pastry bag or gallon-sized sealable storage bag. Snip off the end of the bag to make an opening about ¾-inch wide. Perch the bag on the edge of the large saucepan of simmering water and squeeze dough through the opening, using floured kitchen scissors or a table knife to cut bite-size nuggets (about 1 inch) directly into the water. If you're worried you'll overcook some before you have time to pipe out all the dough, don't be a hero. Pipe as many as you can in about 60 seconds, then stir gently and cook until the gnocchi float to the surface, 2 to 3 minutes. Transfer one gnocchi to the bowl of cold water to cool slightly and taste to check for doneness. If needed, continue simmering the remaining gnocchi for 1 to 2 minutes more.

(recipe continues)

STAUB

TAKEAWAYS

- For a simpler dish, try the gnocchi with your favorite pesto or tomato sauce, or simply toss with some butter, grated Parmigiano, and a few grinds of black pepper.
- Simmer—don't boil—the gnocchi. Pâte à choux is delicate, and a rolling boil can tear the nuggets and make them tough on the outside while raw inside. A steady simmer puffs them up at just the right pace, so they cook through while staying fluffy.
- With flour-based dough instead of the usual potato-based, the gnocchi can be drained and held for 10 to 15 minutes while you make the sauce, if you transfer them from the colander to the cooling pan right away so they don't stick.
- To make French gnocchi ahead of time, poach, drain, and toss them with olive oil on a parchment-lined baking sheet. They can be held at room temperature for up to 2 hours or refrigerated, uncovered, until cold, then covered and chilled for up to 24 hours. When ready to serve, brown them straight from the fridge in a hot skillet with a little oil until crisp and heated through.

Scoop out and reserve about 1¼ cups of the cooking water. Using a wire spider or slotted spoon, transfer the gnocchi to a parchment-lined baking sheet, toss with oil, and spread in a single layer to rest while you make the sauce (see Takeaways for more on holding cooked gnocchi).

Start the carbonara sauce: In a very large skillet over medium heat, cook the pancetta in 1 tablespoon of the oil, stirring occasionally until golden and crisp, about 8 minutes (don't rush it). Remove the skillet from the heat. Using a slotted spoon, transfer the pancetta to paper towels to drain. Set aside the skillet with the rendered fat.

When ready to serve, heat the remaining 2 tablespoons oil in another very large skillet over medium-high heat. Add the gnocchi and cook, undisturbed, until the undersides are browned, 2 to 3 minutes. Stir gently and continue cooking until lightly browned all over and heated through, 2 to 3 minutes more. Remove the skillet from heat (this is important!).

If the pancetta fat in the skillet has solidified, warm it over medium heat to melt. Pour the fat over the gnocchi, add the cheese with about ⅓ cup of the warm pasta cooking water, and stir to melt the cheese.

Drop the egg yolks in the center of the gnocchi and mix, letting the skillet's residual heat warm the yolks to thicken the sauce, then add enough pasta water to make it creamy. Stir in the pancetta and season with pepper. Transfer to bowls and serve with additional Parmigiano on the side for grating.

The Creamiest, Cheesiest Mac and Cheese

Lots of macaroni and cheese recipes are baked, but my stovetop approach unleashes the silkiest, smoothest noods. If the lumps in typical cheese sauces bother you (they bother me), there is a hack. The gritty texture is caused by the cheese proteins "cooking" from excessive heat. The fix is adding vinegar and baking soda to the milk to react with the cheese and keep those proteins from turning into little meat loaves.

Serves 6

8 ounces (2 cups) elbow macaroni

⅓ cup distilled white vinegar

1¼ teaspoons baking soda

1½ cups whole milk

4 ounces cream cheese, cut up

2 teaspoons unseasoned rice vinegar

1 pound sharp white cheddar cheese, shredded (see Takeaways)

Kosher salt

Hot sauce (optional)

Bring a large saucepan of salted water to a boil over high heat. Add the macaroni and cook according to the package directions just until almost tender (al dente); don't overcook. Drain well.

Make the sauce: Meanwhile, combine the white vinegar and baking soda in a medium saucepan and whisk until it stops foaming. Whisk in the milk and bring to a simmer over medium heat. Remove from the heat and add the cream cheese and rice vinegar. With an immersion blender, process until smooth. Gradually add the cheddar, blending each addition until smooth before adding more cheese. Season with salt and hot sauce, if using.

Stir in the macaroni and reheat, stirring often, for 1 to 2 minutes over medium heat. Serve immediately.

Baked Mac and Cheese Slices: For a cool presentation (and for those of you who love the browned, chewy bits on baked mac and cheese), use this "slice and bake" method of serving: Line an 8½ x4½-inch loaf pan with a large sheet of plastic wrap, letting the plastic droop over the sides. Pour the cooked macaroni and cheese into the pan and cover with the overhanging plastic wrap. Refrigerate until chilled and firm, at least 3 hours, or up to 2 days. Invert and unmold the macaroni and cheese onto a carving board, discarding the wrap. Cut into six to eight slices.

Preheat the oven to 350°F. Melt 4 tablespoons (½ stick) unsalted butter. Line a large baking sheet with parchment paper and brush with some of the butter. Arrange the slices on the sheet and brush generously with the remaining butter. Bake until golden brown and heated through, about 25 minutes. (Leftover slices keep well, covered and refrigerated, for up to 3 days. Reheat on a parchment-lined baking sheet in a 350°F oven until hot and crisped, about 10 minutes.)

TAKEAWAYS

- For the best mac and cheese, use a quality cheese. Never buy pre-shredded—it's coated with anti-caking agents to keep the shreds separated, so it never melts as well as cheese you shred yourself. Use the large holes on a box grater or a food processor's shredding disk.
- Use this recipe whenever you need a fantastic cheese sauce. You can use other cheese, such as Gruyère, or a combination of cheddar and Gruyère. The cheese sauce can be transferred to a covered container, cooled, and refrigerated for up to 5 days. Before using, reheat gently in a saucepan over medium-low heat, stirring often, until hot and melted.

Spicy Cold Korean Noodles

Known as *bibim guksu* (spicy noodles) in Korea, these cold noodles are usually vegan, but you can protein up the summer staple with shrimp, shredded chicken, or a fried egg on top. It's not just popular in hot weather because it's cold. Koreans have a practice of fighting fire with fire, eating spicy food to bring their life force in line with the season's heat. While the sauce is fiery, its sweet ingredients help calm things down. Surprised to see soda in there? It adds acidity and carbonation to brighten, lighten, and smooth the dish.

Serves 4

10 ounces somen noodles

⅓ cup gochugaru (Korean chili flakes)

⅓ cup gochujang (Korean chili paste)

⅓ cup granulated sugar

⅓ cup plus 1 tablespoon cider vinegar

½ eating apple (such as Gala), cored and chopped (about 1 cup)

⅓ cup light-colored soft drink (such as lemon-lime soda or ginger ale)

2 cloves garlic, crushed and peeled

1 slice canned pineapple, plus 3 tablespoons pineapple juice from can

About 1 cup kimchi, for serving

Seaweed flakes (such as nori), for serving

Sesame seeds, for sprinkling

Bring a large saucepan of water to a boil over high heat. Add the somen and cook, stirring often to be sure they don't stick together, until al dente, about 3 minutes. Drain and rinse well under cold running water. Return to the pot and fill it with ice water. Let the noodles stand to chill while making the sauce.

Whisk the gochugaru, gochujang, sugar, and vinegar together in a small bowl. In a blender, process the apple, soft drink, garlic, and pineapple and pineapple juice until smooth. Add the chili mixture and process to combine.

Lightly drain the noodles, leaving some of their water clinging. Transfer to a bowl and toss with half of the sauce. Divide among four to six serving bowls. Top each with a portion of kimchi and sprinkle with seaweed flakes and sesame seeds. Serve cold, passing the remaining sauce at the table for anyone who wants extra heat.

TAKEAWAYS

- Somen are thin Japanese wheat noodles similar to Italian vermicelli, which can be a substitute here. Adjust the cooking time as needed to cook the vermicelli until it's tender.
- It's common in Korean cold noodle dishes to make more sauce than you'll need; the noodles should be glossy, not drowning. The extra keeps well in the refrigerator for up to a week and is great spooned over rice bowls, grilled meats, or even scrambled eggs.

Brother Vincent's Flying Noodles with Shrimp in Lobster Sauce

Like me, Vincent Lim was known as a restaurant chef before he broke out as a content creator (@dimsimlim). He's based in Australia, but we both grew up in Texas, and we both cook from a deeply nostalgic place while embracing the viral new-new. Two things to know about this very viral dish: First, it's probably the coolest way to serve noodles. Second, prep is everything, because you need to move quickly on the shrimp and sauce after frying the noodles so they don't get cold. This is based on Vincent's recipe, and it's an adventure with a rad result.

Serves 4

Flying Noodles

2 cups neutral cooking oil (such as avocado or canola), for frying

12 ounces fresh stir-frying noodles (such as lo mein, see Takeaways), uncooked

Shrimp in Lobster Sauce

2 tablespoons fermented Chinese black beans, soaked in warm water for 10 minutes (optional)

3 cups Chicken Stock (page 222, or use canned)

2 tablespoons Chinese rice wine, dry sherry, or sake

½ teaspoon granulated sugar

½ teaspoon freshly ground white pepper

¼ teaspoon MSG (optional)

3 tablespoons cornstarch

2 tablespoons neutral cooking oil (such as avocado or canola)

2 tablespoons minced, peeled fresh ginger

2 cloves garlic, minced

8 ounces peeled and deveined jumbo (21–25 count) shrimp, cut in half lengthwise

2 scallions, white and green parts, cut into 2-inch lengths

1 large egg white, lightly beaten

Toasted sesame oil

Fresh cilantro leaves, for serving

Lime rounds, for serving

Fry the noodles: Heat the oil in a medium saucepan over medium heat until it registers 350°F on an instant-read thermometer. Reduce the heat to keep the oil at the correct temperature. Line a deep serving bowl with paper towels.

Place an empty large skillet or wok on the stove near the oil. Loosen up the noodles and add to the skillet, leaving them in a pile. Turn the stove burner to medium. Working quickly, use heatproof tongs to lift and twist the noodles into a standing 7-inch column still connected to the base. Insert two chopsticks into the top of the column in their natural holding position. Using one hand to hold the chopsticks in place, gradually pour the hot oil from the saucepan down the column to fry the noodles and the pile below. Continue until all the oil is in the skillet.

Using a ladle, continue to spoon the hot oil over all the noodles (top first) until golden brown and crisp, about 3 minutes. The chopsticks should stay in place. Using a slotted spatula, carefully lift the noodle cake and place on the paper towels in the serving bowl to drain.

Make the shrimp in lobster sauce: If using the black beans, drain, pat dry, and roughly smash under a large knife. Mix the stock, rice wine, sugar, white pepper, and MSG (if using) in a small bowl. Add the cornstarch and whisk to combine. Add the black beans and set aside.

Heat a second large skillet or wok over high heat. Add the oil and heat until hot but not smoking. Stir in the ginger and garlic and cook until fragrant, about 15 seconds. Add the shrimp and cook, stirring almost constantly, until they turn opaque, about 1½ minutes. Stir in the scallions. Give the stock mixture a stir to redissolve the cornstarch on the bottom, add to the skillet, and bring to a boil to thicken. While stirring, add the egg white and let it set into shreds, about 10 seconds. Remove from the heat and drizzle with sesame oil.

Discard the paper towel from the noodle bowl, leaving the noodle base in the bowl. Pour the shrimp in lobster sauce on the noodles and sprinkle with the cilantro.

To serve, break up the noodles with a large spoon and stir them into the sauce. Spoon into bowls and serve with the limes.

TAKEAWAYS

- Fresh lo mein noodles are sold at Asian markets in the refrigerated section. If you can't find them, look for fresh Chinese egg noodles, ramen, or yakisoba—all have a similar chew and fry up crisp.

- Don't feel like making the "flying" noodles? No problem. Make a fried noodle cake: Line a large baking sheet with paper towels. Heat ½ cup neutral oil in a large skillet over medium-high heat until the oil is shimmering. Spread the fresh noodles in a thick bed in the oil and fry until crisp golden brown on the underside, about 3 minutes. Using two wooden spoons, carefully flip the noodle bed and continue frying until the other side is golden brown, 2 to 3 minutes more. Using spoons or tongs, move the noodle bed to the paper towels to drain. Transfer to a deep platter. Make the shrimp and sauce, pour on the noodle bed, and serve.

Okonomiyaki with Bacon

Okonomiyaki is a late-night comfort for me. The savory pancake is an Okinawan specialty, and its name breaks down to *okonomi* (whatever you like) *yaki* (grilled). That says it all. Cabbage is the traditional base, but you can play with all kinds of veggies and proteins. Whatever your "whatever" is, it'll be good with bacon.

Makes 2 pancakes
(serves 4 to 6)

Simple Dashi

1¼ cups boiling water

1 tablespoon Hondashi bonito soup stock

Pancakes

½ cup unbleached all-purpose flour

1 teaspoon shichimi togarashi

½ teaspoon baking powder

Pinch of kosher salt

1 large egg

4 cups sliced green cabbage

4 slices standard-cut bacon, cut in half to make 8 pieces

Neutral cooking oil (such as avocado or canola), as needed for the pancakes

To Serve

Tonkatsu sauce (such as Bulldog brand), in a squeeze bottle for drizzling (or see Takeaways)

Mayonnaise (such as Kewpie)

Bonito flakes (optional)

4 scallions, white and green parts, thinly sliced

Make the dashi: Stir together the boiling water and Hondashi in a small bowl and let cool.

Make the pancakes: Whisk the flour, togarashi, baking powder, and salt together in a medium bowl. Add the dashi and egg and whisk until smooth—it should look like a moderately thick pancake batter; add more water if needed. Add the cabbage and mix well so the batter is coating all the cabbage.

Put four bacon pieces in a nonstick skillet and place over medium-high heat (they will render and crisp as the pancake cooks; if you prefer thick-cut bacon, par-cook lightly first so the fat fully renders). Stir the cabbage mixture again and add half to the skillet, covering the bacon. Spread the cabbage to about ½-inch thickness. Using a wooden spatula, push the edges of the pancake in to give it a nice round shape. Drizzle about 2 tablespoons oil around the pancake. Cook until the underside is browned, 4 to 5 minutes. Flip the pancake over and press down with the spatula to help with even cooking. If the pancake seems dry, drizzle more oil around the edges. Cook to brown the other side, 4 to 5 minutes more. Transfer to a platter. Repeat with the remaining ingredients to make a second pancake.

Garnish the pancakes with zigzags of the tonkatsu sauce and mayonnaise, then sprinkle with lots of bonito flakes (if using) and the scallions. Cut into wedges and serve.

TAKEAWAYS

- If you can't find Hondashi (the instant version of dashi, an all-purpose stock made from bonito flakes and kombu seaweed), substitute vegetable or chicken bouillon powder, or even white miso (whisk about 1 teaspoon miso into 1 cup hot water to make a light broth approximating the dashi).
- Tonkatsu sauce, basically a Worcestershire-flavored ketchup with fruit puree, is a classic condiment for okonomiyaki. I use Bulldog brand, but you can easily make your own by whisking together about ½ cup ketchup, 1 tablespoon fruit jelly (preferably apricot, but whatever you have), and 1 teaspoon (or more) Worcestershire sauce.
- No squeeze bottle? Put the tonkatsu sauce in a small resealable plastic storage bag, snip off the corner, and pipe.

Riggi Bolo

A long-simmered Bolognese is something to crave. Speaking of that word, my mentor and brother Nathan Crave is the one who taught me the ways of the sauce in the early days at Palace Kitchen (my favorite restaurant of any I've worked in, and the one that really sparked me as a chef and creator). Nate put it this way: "This shit needs to be cooking for hours, until it looks like a Wendy's Frosty, but a little thinner, and delicious." Nailing it is about finesse, in this case the restrained use of tomato—the meat should be the star. And be sure to serve it with lots and lots of freshly grated Parmigiano.

Serves 4 to 6; makes about 2 quarts sauce (half reserved for another meal)

8 ounces pancetta, cut into 2-inch chunks

1½ pounds ground round (85 percent lean)

8 cloves garlic, crushed under a knife and peeled

1 large yellow onion, coarsely chopped

1 medium carrot, coarsely chopped

1 medium celery stalk, coarsely chopped

2 tablespoons extra virgin olive oil

Kosher salt and freshly ground black pepper

1 (6-ounce) can tomato paste (6 tablespoons)

2 cups dry white wine (such as Pinot Grigio)

1 quart Chicken Stock (page 222, or use canned)

1 quart whole milk

3 tablespoons finely chopped fresh parsley

1 pound rigatoni, cooked according to package directions, drained

Freshly grated Parmigiano-Reggiano (lots and lots), for serving

Arrange the pancetta and ground round in separate areas on a large baking sheet and place in freezer until partially frozen, about 30 minutes. In batches, coarsely grind the pancetta in a food processor. Add an equal portion of the ground round to each batch and pulse together until very finely ground, almost a paste. Transfer to a bowl.

With the food processor running, drop the garlic through the feed tube to mince it. Add the onion, carrot, and celery and pulse until combined and finely minced. Transfer to another bowl.

Heat the oil in a large Dutch oven over medium-high heat. Add the ground meat paste and cook, stirring occasionally and breaking up the meat with the side of a spoon, until it loses its raw look (it doesn't have to brown), about 8 minutes. Season with 2 teaspoons salt and ½ teaspoon pepper. Stir in the minced vegetables and cook, stirring occasionally until the onion is translucent, about 4 minutes. Stir in the tomato paste and mix well. Cook until the liquid is reduced and you can hear the paste sizzling and searing in the pot, about 3 minutes.

Add the wine and stir to loosen any browned bits in the pot. Stir in the stock and milk and bring to a boil. Reduce the heat to low and simmer uncovered, stirring occasionally, until the liquid has reduced to the level of the meat and vegetables, about 4 hours. Add the parsley and season with salt and pepper.

To serve, toss the pasta with half of the sauce (about 1 quart) in a large bowl. Serve hot, with the Parmigiano passed on the side. (The remaining sauce can be cooled, transferred to a covered container, and refrigerated for up to 3 days or frozen for up to 2 months.)

TAKEAWAYS

- I'm grinding the ground round a second time with the pancetta for better flavor and exposure to the seasonings. This makes an especially rich Bolognese.
- You know your favorite pasta and how much sauce you like. I suggest 1 quart sauce for 1 pound dry or fresh pasta, cooked. This sauce freezes well, so like most Italian cooks, I make a big batch to have some for future meals.
- Real Parmigiano-Reggiano (the imported Italian kind, not the American version) is loaded with flavor. Never toss the rinds after you've grated the cheese. Instead, the leftover rinds can have a second life simmering in soups and stocks, where they will release their flavor. In fact, you could add a couple rinds to this Bolognese if you have them and you feel like it.

Italian Grandma Pizza with Pepperoni

I don't have an Italian grandma. If I did, this is the pizza my sweet and resourceful nonna would make. "Grandma pizza" is a specific style of pan pizza that started with Italian immigrants on Long Island making their pies at home. Instead of messing with a peel and shaping the dough into a round, you just stretch it into a sheet pan. Throw the dough together in the morning and let it rise all day for pizza that night.

Serves 6

¼ cup extra virgin olive oil

1 medium yellow onion, finely chopped

2 cloves garlic, minced

1 (28-ounce) can whole Italian plum tomatoes in juice, coarsely chopped (see Takeaways)

¼ cup red wine vinegar

2 teaspoons dried oregano

½ teaspoon crushed red hot pepper

2 tablespoons extra virgin olive oil, for the pan

Semolina or yellow cornmeal, for sprinkling

No-Knead Pizza Dough (page 242), made at least 10 hours before baking

4 cups shredded low-moisture mozzarella

6 ounces thinly sliced pepperoni, cut into thin strips

Make the sauce: Heat the oil in a medium skillet over medium heat. Add the onion and garlic and cook, stirring occasionally, until the onion is translucent, about 4 minutes. Add the tomatoes and their juice, the vinegar, oregano, and hot pepper and bring to a boil. Reduce the heat to low and cook at a brisk simmer, stirring occasionally, until the juices have thickened, about 45 minutes. You should have about 3½ cups sauce. Remove from the heat and let cool. (The cooled sauce can be covered and refrigerated for up to 5 days.)

Position an oven rack in the top third of the oven. If you have one, put a pizza stone on the rack and preheat the oven to 425ºF. Generously grease the bottom and sides of a large baking sheet with the oil. Sprinkle with semolina to coat and tap out the excess. Scrape the dough into the prepared sheet pan. Pat and stretch the dough into an even layer in the pan. (If it resists stretching, cover with a kitchen towel and let stand for about 15 minutes to warm it up.)

Sprinkle the dough with half of the mozzarella, leaving a ½-inch border. Spread the cooled sauce on top. Sprinkle the pepperoni evenly over the sauce, then sprinkle with the remaining mozzarella. Invert a second large baking sheet and use it like a lid to cover the first sheet pan.

If the bottom of your oven is flat (and without a heating element), place the doubled pans directly on the oven floor and bake for 5 minutes. Transfer to the top rack and continue baking for 20 minutes. It not using the oven floor, just bake on the stone for 25 minutes. (If you don't have a pizza stone, preheat the oven as directed and bake directly on the rack in the top third of the oven. The double-pan method will still crisp the crust evenly.)

Using potholders, hold the stacked pans together and remove them from the oven. Carefully lift off the top pan and set it aside—you won't need it again. Increase the temperature to 475ºF and bake until the cheese is bubbling, about 5 minutes. Remove the pan from the oven and let the pizza stand for 3 to 5 minutes. Sprinkle with the basil, cut into rectangles, and serve.

TAKEAWAYS

- You can buy tomatoes already chopped or diced, but they're treated to hold their shape, and you want the fruit to break down during cooking. It's easy to chop up whole tomatoes in the can with their juice. Just take kitchen scissors and go nuts. Then you're ready to pour right into the skillet in step 1.
- The stacked-pan trick is a must for a grandma pizza. The extra heat from the top pan helps the pizza rise more quickly and evenly. If you've ever baked a bread loaf in a covered Dutch oven, it's a similar technique. It also keeps the topping from over-browning during the longish bake. Just be safe when dealing with the hot stacked pans.
- Baking the pizza directly on the oven floor gives it a burst of rising and a crisper bottom by simulating the kind of deck oven that many pizzerias use. Of course, it won't work if your oven has a heating element above the oven floor; in that case you should use a pizza stone (invented for the same purpose of giving home ovens a hot, flat surface for baking pizzas).
- You can use any topping you like for this pizza. Nonna is good with it.

KIMCHUP

Kimchup Fried Rice

Spam and day-old rice are basically my roommates, because they're always in my kitchen. And there are usually multiple batches of kimchi in my fridge, because I love the fermented fizz. That is the foundation of an easy meal that calls back to a late-night special at Palace Kitchen, where we made hot dogs from scratch and served them with kimchup. It's exactly what you think it is, and it will change your life.

Serves 3 to 4

Kimchup

¾ cup ketchup

¼ cup kimchi, plus 2 tablespoons kimchi juice

1 teaspoon soy sauce

Fried Rice

2 tablespoons neutral cooking oil (such as avocado or canola)

1 cup diced Spam or cooked ham

2 scallions, white and pale green part only, finely chopped (reserve green parts for garnish)

4 cloves garlic, minced

4 cups cold cooked rice, preferably day-old short-grain (sushi) rice

Kosher salt and freshly ground black pepper

1 large egg

To Serve

Shichimi togarashi

Kewpie mayonnaise

2 scallions, green parts only, cut into thin rounds

Make the kimchup: Process the ketchup, kimchi and its juice, and soy sauce in a mini food processor (or in a small bowl with an immersion blender) until smooth. Transfer to a covered container. (Makes about 1 cup, and you'll only need half for this recipe. The kimchup can be refrigerated for up to 2 weeks but will be stronger in flavor as it ferments.)

Make the fried rice: Heat a large skillet over medium-high heat. Add 1 tablespoon of the oil and heat until very hot. Add the Spam, white and pale green chopped scallion, and garlic and cook, stirring often, until the onion softens, about 3 minutes. Crumble in the cooked rice and cook, stirring often, until hot, about 3 to 5 minutes. Stir in ½ cup kimchup and cook until the rice is evenly coated and lightly caramelized, about 1 minute more. Season with salt and pepper. Transfer to a serving bowl.

Wipe out the skillet with paper towels. Add the remaining 1 tablespoon oil and heat over medium-high heat until shimmering. Crack the egg into the skillet and fry until sunny side up, with edges that are crispy and a white that is set, about 2 minutes. Put the egg on the rice. Sprinkle the fried rice and egg with togarashi. Squeeze a zigzag of mayonnaise on top and sprinkle with the green scallion rounds. Serve hot.

TAKEAWAY

- Korean cooks love Spam, and that's what I use. But basic ham is good, too, or even the meat from a leftover pork chop.

Chapter 5

Sandos, Burgers, and Tacos

Toasted Cheese Sandwich

This is grilled cheese purified—nothing but sharp white cheddar melted on sourdough toasted with butter. The salty tang of the cheese against perfectly caramelized bread is dank on its own, but you can add fruity umami with the Savory Strawberry Jam in the Takeaways.

Serves 2

4 slices crusty sourdough bread, cut ¼-inch thick

4 tablespoons softened butter, divided

6 ounces sharp white cheddar cheese, thinly sliced, divided

Heat a very large skillet or griddle over medium heat. Put the bread in the skillet to warm just the undersides (see Takeaways), about 1 minute.

For each sandwich, put 2 bread slices, warm side up, on the work surface. Put half the cheese on the warm side of one slice and top with the warm side of another slice (if using the strawberry jam, spread some on the warm side of the second slice before sandwiching). Spread 1 tablespoon of the butter on the top of the sandwich and set aside. Repeat to make the second sandwich.

Place the sandwiches in the skillet, butter side down, and top with a flat plate or skillet lid. Cook, adjusting the heat as necessary so the sandwiches don't brown too quickly, until the undersides are golden brown, about 2 minutes. Spread the tops of the sandwiches with the remaining butter. Flip them over and top with the plate. Continue cooking until the bread is golden brown and the cheese is melted, about 2 minutes more. Cut the sandwiches in half and serve immediately.

TAKEAWAYS

- Warming the sourdough in the dry skillet first is a simple restaurant trick. It gives the bread a head start, guarding against the grilled sandwiches having scorched outsides and cold centers.
- To make about 1½ cups Savory Strawberry Jam, you'll need 1 pound of berries (hulled and quartered), 1 cup sugar, ¼ cup fresh lemon juice, 1 tablespoon soy sauce, 1½ teaspoons guajillo powder, and 1 teaspoon sumac. Combine all ingredients in a medium, nonreactive saucepan and let stand until the berries release some juices, about 15 minutes. Bring to a simmer, stirring often to be sure the fruit isn't scorching, until the juices are thickened and syrupy, about 35 minutes (if you're not sure on the thickness, use the chilled saucer test on page 204). Let cool. Transfer to a covered container and refrigerate until chilled and thickened, at least 3 hours or overnight. (The jam can be refrigerated for up to 3 weeks.)

Pimiento Smash Burgers

Great Seattle burgers are regular stars of my Instagram Stories, from the tavern burger at Loretta's Northwesterner to the smashburger at Familyfriend. When I make my own, I like the smash method because of the tasty crust that comes from searing a super-thin patty on a super-hot skillet. Ground chuck brings the juiciness, and pimiento cheese adds sloppy-good contrast. But toppings don't make a burger. Just cook it right. That's the whole game.

Serves 4

1¼ pounds ground chuck

1½ teaspoons kosher salt

½ teaspoon freshly ground black pepper

1 tablespoon neutral cooking oil (such as avocado or canola)

8 tablespoons Pimiento Cheese (page 30)

4 brioche buns, split

Thinly sliced yellow or white onion, for serving

Condiments such as ketchup and mustard, for serving

Preheat the oven to its lowest setting (about 100°F). Shape the ground chuck into eight equal portions, shape into balls, then press to make eight thin patties 3 to 4 inches in diameter. Season all over with the salt and pepper.

Use a wad of paper towels to wipe the oil over a large, heavy skillet (or a griddle, preferably cast-iron) that is large enough to hold four patties without crowding. Heat over high heat until very hot—it's okay if the oil smokes a little. Add four of the patties and cook for 1 minute. Using a metal spatula, firmly press each patty to "smash it," and cook until the undersides are crisp and browned, about 1 minute longer. (The thin burgers will be almost cooked through at this point.) Flip the patties and cook to brown the other sides, about 1 minute more. Transfer to a broiler pan and keep warm in the oven. Cook the remaining four patties in the same way, but top each with 2 tablespoons of the cheese during the last minute of cooking. Add to the broiler pan in the oven and keep warm.

In batches, add the buns to the skillet, cut-side down, and cook until lightly toasted, about 1 minute. For each burger, place a plain patty on a roll bottom, top with a cheesed patty, and add some onion slices. Cap with the roll top and serve immediately, with whatever condiments you're using.

TAKEAWAY

● Know what makes a better burger? Simply seasoning the outside of the meat and not kneading it through. The seasoning on the surface brings out juices that cook into a fantastic crust when the patty hits the skillet.

Creamy Chicken Tortas

In the Rio Grande Valley, where I grew up, flea-market tortas are the best ones—greasy rolls stuffed with queso fresco and *deshebrado* (shredded) chicken. The lady who ran my favorite stand in town was arrested for bringing in illegal Mexican cheese, which tasted so right. But thankfully she's back in business. This tribute makes moist chicken that you shred and snuggle into avocado slices and creamy Cotija Dressing on a crusty roll. Not as greasy, but straight from my Brownsville heart.

Serves 4

8 bone-in, skin-on chicken thighs (about 7 ounces each)

1 medium yellow onion, cut into half-moons

1 teaspoon kosher salt

3 cloves garlic, crushed

1 jalapeño chile, cut into rounds (including seeds), plus more for serving

1 teaspoon dried oregano, preferably Mexican, crumbled

4 sprigs fresh cilantro, plus more for serving

5 black peppercorns

4 crusty oblong sandwich rolls (see Takeaways), split

Cotija Dressing (page 233)

1 Hass avocado, pitted and cut lengthwise into 12 thin slices

Hot sauce (such as Valentina), for serving

Put the chicken thighs, onion, and salt in a large saucepan and add enough water to cover. Bring to a boil over high heat, skimming off any foam on the surface. Add the garlic, jalapeño, oregano, cilantro, and peppercorns and reduce the heat to low. Simmer, partially covered, for 25 minutes, until the chicken is just cooked through. Remove from the heat, cover tightly, and let stand for 20 to 30 minutes so the meat finishes gently and stays tender. Transfer the thighs to a plate and let cool. (Reserve the broth for another use, such as cooking rice, simmering beans, or starting a soup.)

When the chicken is cool, remove the meat, discarding or reserving the skin and bones. Transfer the meat to a bowl and shred with two forks or your fingers. (Or shred with a stand mixer; see Takeaways.)

Position a broiler rack about 6 inches from the source of heat. Place the rolls, split sides up, on a broiler pan and broil until lightly toasted, about 1 minute. For each sandwich, spread a roll generously with dressing. Add one-quarter of the shredded chicken to the bottom half of the roll. Top with three avocado slices, a few cilantro sprigs, and some jalapeño rounds. Cap with the roll top, cut in half, and serve with the hot sauce.

TAKEAWAYS

- You can substitute any cooked chicken (including a rotisserie bird) for the home-cooked version. You'll need about 3 cups.
- The easiest and most efficient way to shred chicken is with a stand mixer. Just put the meat in the bowl and beat with the paddle attachment on medium speed until shredded, about 1 minute. Don't mix too long, though, or you'll end up with mashed chicken.
- The roll for a torta could be a *telera* (long with three sections) or *bolillo* (like a football with pointy ends). Both have thin crusts and tender insides, and both are sold at *panaderias* (Mexican bakeries) and Mexican markets. Any crusty, oblong sandwich roll will do, though.
- This sandwich goes great with escabeche, a blend of pickled vegetables like carrots, jicama, onions, radishes, and jalapeños. You'll find it at the same grocery stores that sell torta breads.

Nashville Chicken Banh Mi

I cook from a place of wanting to learn everything I can from everyone I can. So I've picked up flavors and techniques from everywhere, and I'm always seeing parallels and ways to mix iconic stuff that still honor the foundations. Take this banh mi. The Vietnamese sandwich has creamy liver pâté lining the bread like it has in Saigon since the '50s, along with Nashville hot chicken, which is just the thing to cut that silky fat with big, sweet heat. You like what you like, but try to resist the urge to tap in basic mayo for the pâté.

Serves 4

Chicken and Brine

1 cup buttermilk

1 tablespoon kosher salt

1 teaspoon hot sauce (such as Valentina or Tabasco)

4 boneless, skinless chicken thighs (about 5 ounces each)

Hot Honey

¼ cup duck fat, lard, rendered bacon fat, or unsalted butter

1 tablespoon light brown sugar

1 teaspoon cayenne pepper

1 teaspoon sweet paprika

½ teaspoon garlic powder

¼ cup honey

Dredge

2 cups unbleached all-purpose flour

½ cup yellow cornmeal

2 tablespoons kosher salt

2 tablespoons freshly ground black pepper

2 tablespoons sweet paprika

1 tablespoon garlic powder

1 tablespoon onion powder

Neutral cooking oil (such as avocado or canola), for frying

8 thick slices rich bread, preferably milk bread (shokupan), or a brioche loaf

8 ounces store-bought spreadable pâté, such as chicken liver mousse; or liverwurst (braunschweiger)

Banh Mi Pickles (page 228), drained, for serving

Thinly sliced red onion, for serving

Fresh cilantro sprigs, for serving

Brine the chicken: Whisk the buttermilk, salt, and hot sauce together in a medium nonreactive bowl. Add the chicken, cover, and refrigerate for 2 to 4 hours.

Make the hot honey: Melt the fat in a small saucepan over medium heat. Stir in the brown sugar, cayenne, paprika, and garlic powder and cook until fragrant, about 15 seconds. Stir in the honey and let it melt. Remove from the heat. (If the honey cools and solidifies, reheat it gently over low heat.)

Make the dredge: Whisk the flour, cornmeal, salt, pepper, paprika, garlic powder, and onion powder in a medium bowl.

Fry the chicken: One at a time, remove a chicken portion from the brine, shake off the excess, and add to the dredge. Turn to coat well, squeezing the thighs so the dredge adheres (see Takeaways), and place on a large baking sheet. Let stand for a few minutes to set the coating.

Set a wire cooling rack in another baking sheet. Pour enough oil into a large, heavy skillet (preferably cast-iron) to come 1 inch up the sides. Heat over high heat until the oil registers 350°F on an instant-read thermometer. Add the chicken to the pan and fry until the undersides are golden brown, about 3 minutes. Flip the chicken over and fry until the other sides are golden brown and the chicken is cooked through, about 3 minutes more. Transfer to the rack.

Pour the warm hot honey over the chicken on the rack, letting the excess drip off. For each sandwich, spread one bread slice with a quarter of the pâté. Place a chicken thigh on the pâté. Top with pickles, a few cilantro sprigs, and red onion slices. Cap with a second bread slice, cut the sandwich in half, and serve immediately.

TAKEAWAYS

- The buttermilk brine tenderizes the chicken while also giving a deep inner seasoning. If you're in a rush, reduce the time to 1 hour, but don't skip brining entirely.
- The seasoned flour/cornmeal is a super-useful, all-purpose dredge for all kinds of chicken, chops, and fish. I've worked in many restaurants where this mix is always on hand. For crispy fried chicken, rolling the chicken in some flour is not enough. You need to really squeeze the thighs, working the coating into the meat surface. That helps it bond and form a microtextured crust, so it fries up shatter-crisp instead of patchy or soggy.

Nashville Chicken Banh Mi

Concha Breakfast Sandwiches with Chorizo and Egg

This sandwich happened because I was trying to make something trashy. Like, how do I take a pastry that's already kinda bad for you and make it worse in a delicious way? It's the same idea as stuffed French toast—a fork-and-knife breakfast of indulgence. *Conchas* (shells in Spanish, as the sweet bread looks like a shell with its crust of patterned sugar) are the base for a savory bomb of chorizo and egg. Slightly stale is best for the bread, so it can hold up to being soaked in eggs, cream, and more sugar. You're welcome.

Serves 2

Conchas

2 conchas or brioche buns, preferably slightly stale

2 large or extra-large eggs

2 tablespoons granulated sugar

1⅓ cups half-and-half or light cream

Finely grated zest of ½ orange plus ¼ cup juice

½ teaspoon vanilla extract

Pinch of kosher salt

1 tablespoon unsalted butter

Filling

12 ounces Homemade Chorizo (page 225), or store-bought soft chorizo with casings removed

2 slices American cheese

2 large, extra-large, or jumbo eggs

Kosher salt and freshly ground black pepper

Warm maple syrup, for serving (optional)

Prepare the conchas: Preheat the oven to 200ºF. Split the conchas crosswise (brioche buns are likely to be split already). Whisk the eggs and sugar in a large bowl. Add the half-and-half, orange zest and juice, vanilla, and salt and whisk to combine. Add the conchas and let stand to soak, turning to coat both sides, while preparing the skillet.

Melt the butter in a large nonstick skillet or griddle over medium heat. Add the soaked conchas, cut sides down, and cook, adjusting the heat as needed so they don't cook too quickly, until the undersides are browned, about 2 minutes. Flip the conchas and cook to brown the other sides, about 2 minutes more. Transfer to a large baking sheet and keep warm in the oven while preparing the filling.

Cook the chorizo and egg filling: Shape the chorizo into two patties about 5 inches wide (to fit the concha bottoms). Add the patties to the skillet or griddle and cook over medium heat until the undersides are browned, about 2½ minutes. Flip the patties and cook until the other sides are browned and the chorizo is cooked through, about 2½ minutes longer. During the last minute of cooking, top each with an American cheese slice. Using a slotted spatula, transfer each patty to a concha bottom, leaving the fat in the skillet, and keep warm in the oven.

Crack the eggs into the fat in the skillet and season with salt and pepper. Cover and cook until the whites are set but the yolks are still runny, about 1 minute. Top each patty with a fried egg. Cap with the concha top and serve immediately with the syrup (if using) and a fork and knife.

TAKEAWAYS

- You'll find conchas at Mexican markets or *panaderías*. They have a distinctive sugary top crust with ridges like a seashell, but brioche hamburger buns work, too. In either case, the bun should be slightly stale. If you know you're making a sandwich in the morning, let the concha or bun stand at room temperature, uncovered, overnight.
- Conchas can be wide, so make the chorizo patties to fit the bun and adjust the cooking time (the patties should be well done) according to the thickness. Because of the concha's size, you also might want to use extra-large eggs for both the soaking liquid and the fried eggs, or use three large eggs in the soaking liquid and even two large eggs for each sandwich.

Shrimp Po'Boys with Hella Sauce

Po'boys are about hella everything, from flavor to the fact that they're stuffed to overflowing. So I made a sauce with that essence for the ultimate hero sandwich. New Orleans has shops that sell nothing but po'boys, and fried shrimp is one of the most popular fillings for good reason. Here, they get a beer batter that plays extremely well with pickle-y, garlicky, spicy Hella Sauce.

Serves 4

Hella Sauce

½ cup mayonnaise

¼ cup buttermilk

2 tablespoons finely chopped dill pickle

1 tablespoon finely chopped fresh dill

¼ teaspoon onion powder

¼ teaspoon garlic powder

¼ teaspoon hot sauce

Beer Batter Shrimp

1 cup unbleached all-purpose flour

¼ cup cornstarch

½ teaspoon kosher salt

¼ teaspoon freshly ground black pepper

¾ cup chilled lager beer

1 large egg

Neutral cooking oil (such as avocado or canola), for frying

1 pound medium (21–25 count) shrimp, peeled and deveined

Shichimi togarashi, for serving (optional)

4 crusty soft rolls, split lengthwise

1 cup shredded iceberg lettuce, for serving

1 large tomato, cut into thin wedges, for serving

Lemon wedges, for serving

Make the sauce: Whisk the mayonnaise, buttermilk, pickles, dill, onion powder, garlic powder, and hot sauce in a small bowl. Cover and refrigerate until ready to serve. (The sauce can be refrigerated for up to 3 days.)

Make the batter: Whisk the flour, cornstarch, salt, and pepper in a medium bowl. Whisk the beer and egg in another bowl, pour into the flour mixture, and whisk just until the batter has a thick paste-like consistency.

Preheat the oven to 200ºF. Set a wire cooling rack in a large baking sheet.

Pour enough oil into a deep skillet to come halfway up the sides, then heat over medium-high heat until the oil is shimmering. To test the oil, dip one shrimp in the batter to coat, then dip one end into the oil—it should bubble immediately. If not, heat the oil longer.

In batches without crowding the skillet, batter the shrimp, add to the oil, and fry, turning as needed, until GBD (Golden Brown Delicious), about 3 minutes. Using a wire skimmer or a slotted spoon, transfer the shrimp to the rack and keep warm in the oven until all the shrimp are fried. If using, sprinkle the togarashi over the shrimp.

For each sandwich, spread a roll with about 3 tablespoons sauce. Fill the sandwich with a handful of the lettuce, one-fourth of the shrimp, and a few tomato slices. Serve immediately with the lemon wedges.

Crab Cake BLTs

I've made thousands of crab cakes, and this BLT is one of my favorite variations ever. It's a thick sammie that encapsulates how I love to eat—fresh but not fancy, fat and salt harmonized, and always a little crunch.

Serves 6

Crab Cakes

1 (1-pound) can lump crabmeat, Dungeness highly preferred (see Takeaways)

½ cup mayonnaise (preferably Kewpie)

½ cup finely diced red bell pepper

2 scallions, white and green parts, chopped

Finely grated zest of 1 lemon

¾ cup panko (Japanese breadcrumbs), plus more for the pan and sprinkling

Kosher salt and freshly ground black pepper

Smoked Paprika and Horseradish Mayonnaise

½ cup mayonnaise

1½ tablespoons prepared horseradish

1 tablespoon fresh lemon juice

2 teaspoons smoked paprika

Kosher salt and freshly ground black pepper

BLTs

6 thick-cut bacon strips

2 tablespoons unsalted butter

6 brioche buns, split and toasted

6 large tomato slices

6 leaves red lettuce

Prepare the crab cakes: Put the crabmeat in a wire strainer and squeeze gently to remove excess liquid. Transfer the crabmeat to a medium bowl. Add the mayonnaise, bell pepper, scallions, lemon zest, and panko and mix just to combine (don't smash it all together). Season with salt and pepper.

Sprinkle a thin layer of panko on the bottom of a baking dish to hold the crabcakes. Using a ½-cup (4-ounce) portion scoop, press about one-sixth of the crabmeat mixture into the scoop to make a half-sphere with a flat bottom and place in the dish. Repeat to make six cakes. Sprinkle more panko over the tops of the crab cakes. Refrigerate uncovered until chilled and set, at least 2 hours or up to overnight.

Reshape the crab cakes: Working with two cakes at a time, press their flat sides lightly together between your cupped hands, then gently round and smooth the sides to form neat domes. Separate the cakes and return to the dish, panko side up. Refrigerate until ready to cook.

Make the smoked paprika and horseradish mayonnaise: Stir the mayonnaise, horseradish, lemon juice, and smoked paprika together in a small bowl. Season with salt and pepper. Cover and refrigerate for 30 minutes, or up to 2 days.

Position a rack in the center of the oven and preheat to 350°F. In a large skillet (preferably cast-iron), fry the bacon over medium heat, turning occasionally, until brown and crisp, about 8 minutes. Transfer the bacon to paper towels to drain, leaving the fat in the skillet.

Add the crab cakes to the fat in the skillet, flat side down, and cook undisturbed until the bottoms are golden brown, about 2 minutes. Flip the cakes and press gently on the tops with the spatula to slightly flatten. Add the butter to the skillet. Transfer the skillet to the oven and bake until the undersides are golden brown and the cakes are heated through, about 10 minutes.

Cut each bacon strip in half. For each sandwich, spread about 2 tablespoons of the mayonnaise on both sides of the bun. Place a crab cake on the bun bottom and top with a tomato slice, a lettuce leaf, and two bacon halves. Cap with the bun top and serve.

TAKEAWAYS

- Fresh crab doesn't necessarily make the best crab cakes. When I get fresh crab, I like to serve it as unadorned as possible to really appreciate the succulent, sweet flavor. Canned crab (sold in 1-pound cans at Costco and other wholesale clubs and many supermarkets) is just fine for crab cakes. Squeezing out the excess canning liquid is an important detail because the liquid dilutes the crab cake flavor, and removing it also makes a firmer cake.
- Don't go nuts with the panko. You want to use just enough inside the crab mixture to hold it together, and only a light sprinkle on the outside for texture—too much in either place will make the cakes heavy and dry.
- Be sure to allow a couple of hours (or more) of refrigeration so the crab cakes can set.

Pimiento Smash Burgers

OG Beef Birria Tacos

OG Beef Birria Tacos

Did I grow up with birria? No. Mexico is a big place, and that particular delicacy didn't bleed into my bit of Texas right across the border. But I am pretty obsessed with it now, the beautiful red flavor of the guajillos and anchos in the broth, and my favorite Oaxaca cheese griddled to the point of becoming like a second taco shell. Birria isn't something you can just whip up, but the slurping crunch of victory is like no other.

Serves 4

Birria Base

7 guajillo chiles, stemmed, seeded, and toasted (see Takeaways)

4 ancho chiles, stemmed, seeded, and toasted (see Takeaways)

Hot water, for soaking

2 medium yellow onions, cut into quarters and broken into layers

12 garlic cloves, peeled

1 tablespoon melted beef tallow or neutral cooking oil (such as avocado or canola)

1 tablespoon coriander seeds

1 tablespoon black peppercorns

3 whole cloves

1 tablespoon dried oregano

1 tablespoon ground ginger

1 teaspoon ground cinnamon

2 chipotle chiles from the can

2 tablespoons fresh lime juice or unseasoned rice vinegar

Birria Beef and Broth

1½ pounds beef chuck roast

Kosher salt

2 tablespoons melted beef tallow or neutral cooking oil (such as avocado or canola)

2 tablespoons tomato paste

Tacos

1 tablespoon beef tallow or neutral cooking oil (such as avocado or canola) for crisping the tortillas (optional)

12 taco-sized (7-inch diameter) corn tortillas

Fresh cilantro leaves

4 cups shredded Oaxaca or Monterey Jack cheese

Lime halves, for serving

Make the birria base: Tear the toasted chiles into large pieces and place in a medium bowl. Add hot water to cover and let stand until softened, 20 to 30 minutes.

Position racks in the top third and center of the oven and preheat the oven to 350°F. Spread the onions and garlic on a large baking sheet and toss with the melted tallow. Place on the top oven rack and bake until roasted and charred on the edges, about 20 minutes. Let cool.

Meanwhile, put the coriander, peppercorns, and cloves on a small baking sheet or oven-proof skillet. Place on the center oven rack and bake until toasted and fragrant, about 5 minutes. Let cool. Transfer the roasted spices to a blender and process until ground. Add the oregano, ginger, and cinnamon and pulse to combine.

Drain the soaked chiles and discard the soaking liquid (which is very bitter). Add the chiles to the blender along with the roasted onions and garlic, the spice mixture, the chipotles, and lime juice. Pour in 1 cup water, cover, and process until the birria base is smooth. (Puree in batches, if necessary.) Transfer the birria base to a large bowl. Add 1 quart water to the blender to rinse out any clinging base and add to the bowl.

Make the birria beef and broth: Season the chuck roast with 2 teaspoons salt. Heat the tallow in a Dutch oven over medium-high heat. Add the chuck roast and cook, turning occasionally, until browned, about 6 minutes. Add the birria base and 1 quart water. Bring to a boil over medium-high heat. Reduce the heat to medium-low, cover tightly, and simmer until the beef is very tender, about 2 hours. Transfer the beef to a large bowl and cool slightly; reserve the braising liquid. Using two forks, shred the beef in the bowl. Cover with foil to keep the filling warm. (The filling can be cooled, covered, and refrigerated for up to 2 days. Reheat in a large nonstick skillet over medium-high heat.)

Whisk the tomato paste into the braising broth and season with salt. Keep the birria broth warm in the Dutch oven over low heat. (The broth can be cooled, covered, and refrigerated for up to 2 days. Before using, reheat over medium-high heat until simmering.)

Make the tacos: Preheat the oven to 200ºF. Line a large baking sheet with parchment paper. Put the shredded beef, tortillas, and cilantro leaves near the stove. Heat a very large nonstick skillet or well-seasoned griddle over medium heat (you may want to use two skillets). If your pan or griddle isn't well-seasoned, brush on some tallow to prevent sticking. In batches, if needed, sprinkle portions of about ⅓ cup of the cheese in 7-inch rounds into the skillet(s). For each taco, quickly dip a tortilla into the broth to coat it and place it on one round of melting cheese. Press on the tortilla with a spatula so the melted cheese oozes to the edges of the tortilla. Add about 3 tablespoons filling in the center of the tortilla and sprinkle with cilantro. Cook until the cheese is melted and the undersides are browned, about 1 minute. Using a spatula, fold each tortilla in half and transfer to the baking sheet. Keep the finished tacos warm in the oven until they are all made.

To serve, spoon the remaining birria broth into small bowls, one for each diner. Transfer the tacos to dinner plates and serve with the lime halves and the broth for dipping.

Octopus Birria Tacos:

Start with a fresh or frozen whole 3-pound octopus, cleaned of its beak and innards. (If frozen, thaw in the refrigerator for about 2 days, as needed.) Bring the birria base to a boil. Holding the octopus by its head, dip the tentacles into the birria base and hold for 10 seconds. Remove and repeat two more times. Submerge the octopus in the base and add enough hot water to cover. Return to a boil and reduce the heat to a simmer. Cook until very tender, about 2 hours. Transfer the octopus to a large baking sheet and let cool. Wrap in plastic wrap and refrigerate until firm and chilled, at least 2 hours or overnight. Cut the tentacles from the body, discard the body, and cut the tentacles into 1-inch chunks. When ready to serve, heat 2 tablespoons olive oil in a large skillet over medium-high heat. Add the octopus and cook, stirring occasionally, until heated through, about 5 minutes. Finish as directed for the beef tacos.

TAKEAWAYS

- To toast dried chiles, use a knife to cut off the stems, split them lengthwise, and trim away the ribs and seeds. Heat a large, heavy skillet or griddle (preferably cast-iron) over high heat. Put the chiles on the skillet and press them down with a spatula or kitchen tongs. Toast them, pressing and flipping occasionally, until they're more flexible and turn darker red, about 1 minute, depending on the heat. Avoid inhaling the fumes from the toasting.
- While some people toast the spices in a skillet, I think it's easy to roast them in the oven at the same time as the onions and garlic. You get a more even toast, too.
- The birria base works with any taco meat. Substitute 2 pounds boneless pork butt or chicken thighs (skin removed but not boned) for the beef. Simmer the pork for about 2 hours, but the thighs for only 45 minutes. My personal favorite is the octopus variation (above), which makes a certified fucking beautiful taco.
- Get creative with the leftover birria broth. For example, add vegetables and beans for a soup. Or freeze it for the next time you want these tacos.

Rio Grande Valley Steak and Avocado Tacos

It used to weird me out when people asked what kind of tacos I grew up with, because tacos were tacos. All I knew was the Matamoros style, rooted in the Mexican town right across the Rio Grande from Brownsville—grilled *bistec* (beefsteak) chopped up to make a filling for tortillas glistening with fat. Avocado, queso fresco, cilantro, and a side of caramelized onions completed the package. I always saved the onions for last and downed them with lime and a shit-ton of salt. My family calls these tacos *piratas*, though no one remembers where the pirate thing came from. They are simple, and perfect.

Serves 4

Quick Caramelized Onions

2 teaspoons neutral cooking oil (such as avocado or canola)

1 large yellow onion, cut into ½-inch rounds

½ teaspoon kosher salt

Steak

2 teaspoons neutral cooking oil (such as avocado or canola)

1 (1⅓-pound) flank steak

Kosher salt and freshly ground black pepper

16 corn "street taco" tortillas (4-inch diameter), warmed (see Takeaways, page 37)

¾ cup crumbled cotija or feta cheese

1½ ripe Hass avocados, pitted, peeled, and cut into 16 slices

Roasted Salsa Verde (page 230), for serving

Cilantro leaves, for topping

Lime wedges, for serving

Cook the onions: Heat the oil in a large skillet over medium-high heat. Add the onions and season with the salt. Cook, stirring occasionally, until they soften and are beginning to brown, 3 to 4 minutes. Add about 3 tablespoons water and stir well with a wooden spatula to loosen the brown layer (fond) of onion juices in the pan. Cook until the liquid evaporates, the onions are sizzling, and another layer of brown fond has formed in the pan, about 2 minutes. Add another 3 tablespoons water, stir well, and cook until the onions are tender and deep beige, about 2 minutes. Reduce the heat to very low and cover to keep warm.

Cook the steak: Heat a large, heavy skillet (preferably cast-iron) over medium-high heat. Add the oil and heat until shimmering. Add the steak and top with a flat pot lid or sandwich press to weigh it down and help give a nice crust to the meat. Cook until the underside is nicely browned, about 4 minutes. Flip the steak and cook to brown the other side, about 4 minutes more for rare steak. Transfer to a carving board and let rest for 5 minutes. Using a sharp knife, cut the meat across the grain (see page 82 for tips) into thin slices, then chop into a ¼-inch dice. Transfer to a bowl and season with salt and pepper.

Warm the tortillas. For each serving, place four warm tortillas on a dinner plate. Fill a tortilla with a portion of the steak, a sprinkle of cheese, a slice of avocado, a spoonful of salsa, and some cilantro leaves. Bring the sides of the tortilla up to hug the filling. Repeat to fill all the tortillas, propping them against each other, filling side up, to stand. Add a portion of the onions to the side of the plate. Serve immediately, with lime wedges and the remaining salsa.

TAKEAWAYS

- Skirt steak is another cut that makes great tacos. The steaks can be long, so you may have to cut a whole steak in half crosswise to fit in the skillet.
- Caramelized onions have a silky texture and sweet-savory flavor that's hard to beat. However, the classic version takes about 45 minutes of slow cooking. It's a lot faster to brown the onions over medium-high heat and occasionally deglaze the skillet to scrape up the concentrated onion juices.

Chapter 6

Sides and Vegetables

Broccolini Shawarma with Spicy Cilantro Raita

Shawarma is one of those spice blends most people have only had on chicken, because of course. But if it tastes good on chicken, then . . . try it on everything. Broccolini is a great vehicle because the seasoning clings, meaning you'll get flavorful and crispy bits through roasting. This dish can be an app, a side, a main (over rice), or pulled into a sandwich. Just stuff a pita with chopped broccolini, raita, diced tomatoes, and shredded crisp lettuce.

Serves 6

Cilantro Raita

1 cup plain Greek yogurt

¼ cup finely chopped fresh cilantro

1 tablespoon minced, seeded serrano or jalapeño chile

2 tablespoons fresh lemon juice

¼ teaspoon crushed hot red pepper

Shawarma Seasoning

1 teaspoon smoked or black peppercorns

1 teaspoon cumin seeds

½ teaspoon coriander seeds

1 teaspoon kosher salt

½ teaspoon ground cinnamon

½ teaspoon ground ginger

½ teaspoon ground turmeric

¼ teaspoon ground allspice

Broccolini

1½ pounds broccolini, trimmed

3 tablespoons extra virgin olive oil

Preheat the oven to 400°F. Heat a large baking sheet in the oven at the same time.

Make the raita: Stir the yogurt, cilantro, serrano, lemon juice, and hot pepper together in a small bowl. Let stand at room temperature to blend the flavors while roasting the broccolini.

Make the seasoning: Heat a small skillet over medium heat until hot. Add the peppercorns, cumin, and coriander and cook, stirring occasionally, until fragrant and smoking, about 2 minutes. Transfer to a plate and let cool. Grind the toasted spices in an electric spice or coffee grinder. Add the salt, cinnamon, ginger, turmeric, and allspice and pulse to combine.

Roast the broccolini: Toss the broccolini with the olive oil in a large bowl. Sprinkle with the seasoning and toss again. Spread on the hot large baking sheet and roast, stirring occasionally, until the stems are tender and the tips are browned and crisp, about 10 to 12 minutes (depending on thickness). For an appetizer, transfer the broccolini to a platter and serve with the raita as a dip. For a side or main, drizzle the raita over the broccolini and serve.

TAKEAWAY

- Broccolini is milder and more tender than standard broccoli, with long, thin stems. Trim off about ½ inch, especially if the ends look dry or woody, leaving the stalks intact for the best presentation (and dipping).

Pan-Roasted Brussels Sprouts with Pancetta and Pear

Brussels sprouts with some form of fatty pork will always be a hit on a menu. In this recipe, you get sweet, salty, tart, and spicy on a green vegetable that makes you feel healthy even with pancetta riding shotgun. What's not to love?

Serves 6

½ cup diced pancetta

1 tablespoon extra virgin olive oil

1 pound Brussels sprouts, trimmed and halved lengthwise

3 tablespoons cider vinegar

1 firm ripe pear (such as red pear or Bosc), unpeeled, cored and diced

2 tablespoons unsalted butter

½ teaspoon kosher salt

¼ teaspoon freshly ground black pepper

⅓ cup coarsely chopped toasted walnuts (see Takeaways)

Cook the pancetta with the oil in a large skillet over medium heat, stirring occasionally, until crisp and browned, about 8 minutes. Do not rush the pancetta. Using a slotted spoon, transfer the pancetta to paper towels to drain, leaving the fat in the skillet.

Increase the heat to medium-high and let the pan heat until the fat is shimmering, about 30 seconds. Add the Brussels sprouts, cut-side down, and cook, without stirring, until deeply browned on the cut sides, about 3 to 4 minutes. Toss and continue cooking, stirring occasionally, until the sprouts are golden brown and tender when pierced with a knife, about 5 minutes more (longer if you like a softer sprout).

Add the vinegar and cook, scraping up any browned bits from the bottom of the pan, until the liquid has mostly evaporated, about 30 seconds. Reduce the heat to medium and add the pears and butter. Cook, stirring gently, until the butter is melted and the sprouts and pears are glossy and sizzling, about 1 to 2 minutes.

Season with the salt and pepper. Add the walnuts and pancetta and toss to combine. Transfer to a serving bowl and serve hot.

TAKEAWAYS

- The biggest mistake people make when cooking Brussels sprouts is not making sure every single one is cut-side down in the skillet (or baking sheet, if you're roasting in the oven) to get the sear. And once they're down, don't touch them until they're caramelized—let them cook.

- Bosc pears are good for this dish because they hold their shape and provide a color contrast to the green sprouts. If you use a more tender variety, like Bartlett or Anjou, just don't use ones that are soft and ripe, as they'll be crushed and mushy by the time the dish is finished.

- To toast walnuts, heat an empty skillet over medium heat. Add the walnuts and cook, stirring occasionally, until fragrant and toasted, about 3 minutes. Keep an eye on them, as they can burn easily. Transfer to a cutting board and let cool before chopping.

STAUB

Charred Broccolini with Cotija Dressing

Charring doesn't just intensify flavor, it adds character and color to a dish—so I'm all about more char, especially on vegetables. You can experiment with other dressings (like the Shallot-Honey Vinaigrette on page 231), but I am partial to my Cotija Dressing on this simple but substantial salad.

Serves 4

12 ounces broccolini, trimmed

1 clove garlic, crushed under a knife and peeled

2 tablespoons extra virgin olive oil

¾ cup Cotija Dressing (page 233), or to taste

3 tablespoons pepitas (skinned pumpkin seeds), toasted (see Takeaway) and coarsely chopped

Flaky salt

In a large bowl, toss the broccolini and garlic with the oil to coat.

Heat a large, heavy skillet (preferably cast-iron) over high heat. Add the broccolini (reserve the garlic) and cook, without stirring, until the underside is charred, about 1½ minutes. Flip the broccolini and cook to char the other side, about 1½ minutes more. Add the garlic and let it brown, about 30 seconds.

Add ¼ cup water and cover tightly. Cook until the liquid evaporates and the broccolini is crisp-tender, about 1 minute. Discard the garlic.

Add as much dressing as you like to the broccolini, and toss. Sprinkle with the pepitas and salt and serve immediately.

TAKEAWAY

- To toast the pepitas, heat a medium skillet over medium heat. Add the pepitas and cook, stirring occasionally, until lightly browned, about 2 minutes. Transfer to a plate to cool.

Chicken-Fried Cauliflower with Green Goddess

You could chicken-fry a shoe and it would be good. That spicy batter is gold. And rich, so it needs the particular balance of green goddess dressing with its fresh, herbaceous brightness (though the Cotija Dressing on page 233 brings a tangier vibe, if that's your thing). This dish works as an app or a side, or a main course if you turn it into tacos—warmed corn tortillas, your favorite salsa, some shredded lettuce, and a drizzle of dressing.

Serves 4 to 6

1 cup buttermilk

2 teaspoons Worcestershire sauce

2 teaspoons kosher salt

½ teaspoon garlic powder

½ teaspoon onion powder

½ teaspoon sweet paprika

½ teaspoon freshly ground black pepper

¼ teaspoon cayenne pepper

1 head cauliflower (about 1 pound), cut into bite-sized florets

Neutral cooking oil (such as avocado or canola), for deep-frying

1 cup unbleached all-purpose flour

¼ cup cornstarch

1 teaspoon baking powder

Lemon wedges, for serving

Carrot-Top Green Goddess Dressing (page 232), for serving

Preheat the oven to 200ºF. Set a wire rack in a large baking sheet.

Whisk the buttermilk, Worcestershire sauce, 1 teaspoon of the salt, the garlic powder, onion powder, paprika, black pepper, and cayenne in a large bowl. Add the cauliflower and stir to coat.

Add enough oil to a large saucepan to come 2 to 3 inches up the sides. Heat over medium-high heat until the oil registers 375ºF on an instant-read thermometer.

Whisk the flour, cornstarch, baking powder, and remaining 1 teaspoon salt in a large bowl. In batches, remove the cauliflower from the buttermilk, letting the buttermilk cling to the florets, and transfer to the flour mixture. Toss to coat. Transfer to the oil and deep-fry until GBD (Golden Brown Delicious), about 3 minutes. Using a wire spider or slotted spoon, transfer to the rack and keep warm in the oven until all the cauliflower is fried.

Pile the cauliflower on a platter and serve hot, with lemon wedges for squeezing and the dressing as a dip.

TAKEAWAYS

- Heating the oil to 375ºF for deep-frying may sound like a high temperature, but when the food is added, the temperature will drop. Be sure to let the oil return to 375ºF when frying subsequent batches.

- The baking powder in the flour will give the fried coating a crisper texture.

Potato Parmesan Gratin Stacks

These are also known as Fancy AF Potatoes, the title of my original YouTube video. The method puts the messiness of scalloped potatoes in stunning order, layered so thin and cut into neat stacks that bring the drama even next to the most beautiful steak. You start by baking a loaf of creamy potato slices that is then chilled to set up, making it easy to cut before baking (or frying) to crispy golden brown. Hundreds of thousands of people watched and learned how to make them, but this detailed guide lives only on the page.

Serves 6

6 tablespoons unsalted butter, melted, plus softened butter for the pan

1 cup heavy cream

1½ teaspoons kosher salt

½ teaspoon freshly ground black pepper

A few gratings of nutmeg

3 large, elongated baking potatoes (such as russet), about 2¼ pounds

¾ cup freshly grated Parmigiano-Reggiano cheese

Neutral cooking oil (such as avocado or canola), for the pan

Flaky salt, for serving

Preheat the oven to 350ºF. Brush the inside of an 8x4-inch metal loaf pan with softened butter. Line the bottom and long sides of the pan with a sheet of parchment paper, letting the excess paper hang over the sides like a sling, and butter the paper with more softened butter. Then melt the 6 tablespoons butter in a small saucepan or in short bursts in the microwave, and set it aside.

Mix the cream, kosher salt, pepper, and nutmeg in a large bowl. Using a mandoline or V-slicer, cut the potatoes lengthwise into very thin slices about 1⁄16-inch thick. As the potatoes are cut, add them to the cream, separating the slices and turning to coat well. One at a time, stack the coated potato slices in the prepared pan, brushing each layer with melted butter, and sprinkling with a teaspoon or two of Parmigiano. Finish with a layer of potatoes and butter. Fold the overhanging parchment paper over to cover the stack. Cover tightly with aluminum foil.

Bake until the potatoes are tender when pierced with a thin sharp knife, about 1 hour. Uncover and let cool completely. Cover again with aluminum foil and refrigerate until chilled, at least 8 hours or overnight.

Preheat the oven to 350ºF. Line a large baking sheet with parchment paper and brush the paper with oil. Briefly place the bottom of the pan on a stove burner on medium-low heat to melt the butter inside the pan, about 1 minute. Run a dinner knife around the inside of the pan. Uncover, lift up on the parchment "handles," and remove the potato loaf from the pan. Discard the parchment. Cut the loaf crosswise into eight equal slices.

Place the potato stacks in the prepared pan. Bake until the undersides are golden brown, 20 to 25 minutes (use a spatula to lift a slice and check). Flip so the browned side faces up, sprinkle the potato stacks with the flaky salt, and serve.

TAKEAWAYS

- While baking is a practical option for serving these, I often fry them up as crispy bites for an appetizer. Preheat the oven to 200ºF. Place a wire cooling rack on a large baking sheet. Cut the unmolded loaf into eight equal slices. Cut each slice crosswise into thirds to make 24 rectangular stacks. Pour enough neutral cooking oil to come about 2 inches up the side of a large saucepan and heat to 350ºF on an instant thermometer. In batches without crowding, fry the potato stacks until golden brown, about 2 minutes. Using a wire spider or slotted spoon, transfer to the rack and keep warm in the oven until all the stacks are fried. Sprinkle with some flaky salt and serve hot.
- The trimmings from the potato loaf can be heated with a little milk and pureed to make a single serving of outrageous mashed potatoes.

Cowboy Beans (Frijoles Charros)

A *charro* is a Mexican cowboy, and the beans named for him are everywhere in my hometown of Brownsville. You'll find them at the taqueria in a bowl, at the barbecue spot in a mug, at family gatherings in a Styrofoam cup, and at Charro Days in everyone's bellies. Charro Days is a weeklong fiesta that takes over the entire town and a nearby chunk of Mexico, and my Uncle Jesse often took home the frijole trophy. This is his recipe—a smoky, zesty, brothy bean "soup" you should eat out of a mug on a cold day. Don't even think about making these with canned beans, as the bean broth is crucial to the ultimate flavor.

Serves 8

1 pound dried pinto beans, rinsed and picked over for stones

8 ounces thick-sliced bacon, coarsely chopped

12 ounces smoked sausage (such as hot links, andouille, or kielbasa), cut into bite-sized pieces

1 large yellow onion, chopped

4 cloves garlic, minced

1 jalapeño chile, cut into rounds (tap out some of the seeds for milder spice)

2 tablespoons freshly ground mixed peppercorns or black pepper

2 tablespoons dried oregano, crumbled

2 teaspoons ground guajillo chile

1 (28-ounce) can Italian plum tomatoes in juice (preferably San Marzano), coarsely chopped, including juices

2 quarts Chicken Stock (page 222, or use canned)

Kosher salt

Coarsely chopped fresh cilantro, for serving

The night before, put the beans in a large bowl and add enough water to cover by 2 inches. Loosely cover the bowl and let stand for at least 8 hours or overnight (refrigerate if the kitchen is warm). Drain well.

Transfer the drained beans to a soup pot and add enough fresh water to cover by 2 inches. Bring to a boil over high heat. Reduce the heat to low and simmer until the beans are almost tender, about 45 minutes, depending on the age of the beans. Set aside and let cool in the pot at room temperature for at least 2 hours. If possible, refrigerate overnight.

Cook the bacon in a large Dutch oven over medium-high heat, stirring often, until the fat is rendered and the bacon is browned, about 10 minutes. Transfer the bacon to paper towels to drain, leaving the fat in the Dutch oven.

Add the sausage to the fat in the pot and cook, stirring occasionally, until beginning to brown, about 3 minutes. Add the onion, garlic, and jalapeño and cook, stirring occasionally, until softened, about 4 minutes. Stir in the pepper, oregano, and ground guajillo and cook until fragrant, about 30 seconds. Add the tomatoes and their juices and stir with a wooden spoon to scrape up the browned bits on the bottom of the pot.

Drain the beans in a colander over a large bowl, reserving the broth for later. Measure and set aside 1 cup of the drained beans. Add the remaining drained beans to the Dutch oven and stir in the reserved bacon, the stock, and 1½ teaspoons salt. Bring to a boil over high heat.

In a blender or food processor, puree the reserved beans with 2 cups of the bean cooking liquid (see Takeaways on page 59 for tips on safe blending). Stir into the pot of beans. Simmer, uncovered, until liquid has reduced by about one-quarter, about 45 minutes. Season with salt. (The beans can be cooled, transferred to covered containers, and refrigerated for 3 days or frozen for up to 3 months.)

Ladle the beans into bowls or mugs, sprinkle with the cilantro, and serve hot.

TAKEAWAYS

- The cooking liquid from the initial simmering of the beans is delicious and useful as a broth for making soups, especially vegetarian ones. You'll have about 4 cups.

- If you have leftover beans, they can be repurposed as refried: Drain the beans and reserve the liquid. For 4 to 6 servings, puree 4 cups beans with an immersion blender in a bowl (or in a food processor), adding enough of the liquid (start with ½ cup) to make a smooth puree. Heat 3 tablespoons lard, duck fat, or neutral cooking oil in a large skillet over medium-high heat. Add the puree and cook until it begins to brown on the bottom, 2 to 3 minutes. Stir and cook until the beans are heated through, about 2 minutes more. Serve plain or with a crumble of queso fresco.

Farro Risotto with Roasted Mushrooms and Squash

Fall brings the wild mushrooms in Seattle, and I make this dish with a mix of whatever looks best at the market (maitakes, chanterelles, and king oysters are my favorites). Don't chop them all crazy—you want to see the different varieties pop against creamy, sage-spiked farro and tender delicata squash.

Serves 4 to 6

Sage Oil

⅓ cup extra virgin olive oil

2 tablespoons coarsely chopped sage leaves and thin stems

Farro

2 cups pearled farro (see Takeaways)

6 cups Vegetable Stock (page 223, or use canned)

2 teaspoons kosher salt

Roasted Vegetables

1 delicata squash (about 1¼ pounds)

4 tablespoons extra virgin olive oil

2 tablespoons maple sugar or light brown sugar

1 teaspoon Aleppo pepper or ½ teaspoon crushed hot red pepper

Kosher salt and freshly ground black pepper

12 ounces assorted mushrooms (such as chanterelle, morel, and maitake; see Takeaways), cut into ½-inch slices

2 cups raw unsalted cashews

1 cup hot water, or as needed

Flaky salt, for serving

Make the sage oil: Heat the oil and sage in a small saucepan over low heat until small bubbles form around the sage, 2 to 3 minutes. Remove from the heat and let steep while making the risotto.

Cook the farro: Bring the farro, stock, and salt to a boil in a medium saucepan over high heat. Reduce the heat to medium-low, cover tightly, and cook until the farro is tender, about 30 minutes. Drain in a wire sieve over a bowl, reserving the stock, and return the farro to the saucepan. Cover and set aside.

Roast the vegetables: Meanwhile, position racks in the upper third and center of the oven and preheat to 400°F. Place a large baking sheet on each rack during preheating.

Cut the squash in half lengthwise and scoop out the seeds. Cut each half again lengthwise to make four wedges. Cut each wedge crosswise into ½-inch slices. Put the squash in a large bowl, drizzle with 2 tablespoons of the oil, the maple sugar, Aleppo pepper, and 1 teaspoon kosher salt, and toss.

Spread the squash flat-side down on the upper hot pan in the oven. Rinse out the bowl. Add the mushrooms, drizzle with the remaining 2 tablespoons olive oil, 1 teaspoon kosher salt, and ¼ teaspoon black pepper, and toss. Spread the mushrooms on the center hot pan. Roast the squash and mushrooms, occasionally stirring the mushrooms, until the vegetables are browned and tender, about 20 minutes. Leave the vegetables in the turned-off oven with the door ajar to keep them warm.

Process the cashews and hot water in a blender (preferably high-powered), until smooth and the consistency of yogurt, adding more water as needed but keeping it on the thick side. Season the cashew cream with kosher salt and pepper.

Add the cashew cream to the farro. Stir over medium heat, adding as much of the reserved farro stock as needed to give the farro a creamy consistency, until hot, about 2 minutes. Stir about half of the mushrooms into the risotto. Season with kosher salt and pepper. Add the squash and the remaining mushrooms. Spoon into soup bowls, drizzle each serving with sage oil, add a sprinkle of flaky salt, and serve immediately.

TAKEAWAYS

- Pearled farro means that the tough outer hull has been removed for faster cooking. If you have whole-grain farro, it'll take closer to an hour to cook.
- Save any mushroom trimmings and use in place of or in addition to the chopped mushrooms in the Vegetable Stock (page 223).
- Delicata squash is a good vegetable to know. Not only is the thin, multicolored skin pretty, it's also edible.
- For an omnivore-friendly version, substitute Chicken Stock (page 222) for the Vegetable Stock and heavy cream for the cashew cream. Sprinkle each portion in its soup bowl with a tablespoon of freshly grated Parmesan before serving.

Korean Korn

Make elote but make it Korean. Because Mexican corn on the cob smothered in mayo and cheese is undefeated, and Korean cheesy corn has a similar soul. You're getting the hotter, cleaner kick of gochujang here, compared with the mild heat of tangy chamoy from the elote I grew up loving. This one blends two of my favorite cuisines, and it's a really different way to enjoy summer corn at its peak.

Serves 4

4 ears corn, husked

3 tablespoons mayonnaise

1 tablespoon gochujang (Korean chili paste)

¼ teaspoon granulated sugar

½ cup shredded and coarsely chopped fresh mozzarella

2 tablespoons unsalted butter, melted

Flaky salt, for serving

Lime wedges, for serving

Put a steamer rack in a large saucepan and add enough water to the pan to almost reach the bottom of the rack. Cover tightly and bring to a boil and build a head of steam. Add the corn on the cob to the rack, cover, and reduce the heat to medium. Steam until the corn is heated through, 8 to 10 minutes. Transfer the corn to a platter and let cool completely. (The corn ears can be wrapped in plastic wrap and refrigerated for up to 2 days.)

Position a broiler rack about 6 inches from the source of heat and preheat the broiler on high.

Mix the mayonnaise, gochujang, and sugar in a small bowl. Slather the cooled corn with the mayonnaise and sprinkle with the cheese, turning to coat the cob all over. Broil, turning occasionally and drizzling with the butter, until the coating is bubbling and browned, 7 to 10 minutes.

Transfer the corn to a platter. Sprinkle with the flaky salt and serve immediately, with the lime wedges for squeezing.

TAKEAWAYS

- For a spicier kick in the mayo, increase the gochujang to 2 tablespoons.
- Chopping previously shredded mozzarella into small bits helps the cheese stick to the mayo better.
- It's essential that the corn is completely cooled before adding the topping. If the corn is hot, the mayo will slide right off.
- I prefer steaming to cook the corn, but it can be grilled. Grill the husked ears over direct medium heat, turning occasionally, until lightly browned and heated through, about 7 minutes. And I'm so serious about letting the corn cool completely before coating.

Tender Biscuits with Honey Butter

Some recipes go straight into my recipe bible as soon as I learn them, including these biscuits. They're designed to be easy—something you pop in the oven for breakfast—and they are simple. But there's one extra step that's worth the slight effort for amazingly tall and fluffy biscuits: folding the dough a few times to create layers in the baked biscuit that just beg for a slathering of honey butter. I also like adding fresh chives for a savory touch.

Serves 8

Biscuits

3 cups unbleached all-purpose flour, plus more for shaping and folding

1 tablespoon baking powder

2 teaspoons kosher sea salt

¾ cup (1½ sticks) cold unsalted butter, cut into ½-inch cubes

¼ cup thinly sliced fresh chives

1¼ cups chilled buttermilk, or as needed

Flaky salt, for topping

Honey Butter

½ cup (1 stick) unsalted butter, softened

⅓ cup honey

Pinch of flaky salt

Make the biscuits: Preheat the oven to 425ºF. Line a large baking sheet with parchment paper or a silicone mat.

Whisk the flour, baking powder, and sea salt together in the bowl of a stand mixer. Add the butter and toss with your hands to coat the cubes. Using your fingers, squish the butter into flakes, being sure to flatten all the cubes. The mixture should look crumbly with some small pieces of butter. Attach the bowl to the mixer and affix the paddle. Mix on low speed, add the chives, then gradually add enough of the buttermilk to make a cohesive dough, leaving 1 or 2 tablespoons buttermilk in the cup. Do not overmix. (Or use an electric mixer to cut in the butter, add the chives, and gradually stir in the buttermilk with a wooden spoon.)

Turn the dough out onto a lightly floured work surface and dust the top with more flour. Pat (or roll) into a 12x6-inch rectangle about ½-inch thick. Fold the dough into thirds like a business letter. Turn the dough so the long open seam faces right. Repeat the shaping and folding two more times. Pat or roll out the dough into a 10x5-inch rectangle about ¾-inch thick, with the long side facing you.

Using a large knife to cut straight down without dragging the knife, cut the dough lengthwise in half, then crosswise into four strips to make eight biscuits. Arrange the biscuits side by side, barely touching, on the prepared baking sheet. Lightly brush the tops with the buttermilk dregs in the cup and sprinkle each with a pinch of flaky salt.

Bake, turning the pan every 4 minutes for even baking, until the biscuits are risen and golden brown and there are no signs of raw dough in the seams, 18 to 20 minutes. Cool on the pan for about 5 minutes, then break the biscuits apart.

Make the honey butter: Meanwhile, mash and mix the butter, honey, and flaky salt in a small bowl with a silicone or rubber spatula until smooth (or beat with an electric hand mixer on medium speed). Keep at room temperature for serving. Serve the biscuits hot, warm, or cooled, with the honey butter.

TAKEAWAYS

- You'll see biscuit recipes that use shortening or lard. I use butter because . . . come on, it's butter and it tastes the best.
- There are also recipes that make a big deal about using low-gluten flour for biscuits. With this much butter (and the buttermilk, which is a tenderizer), the biscuits are going to turn out nice and tender anyway, so no need to shop for a special flour.
- For hot honey butter, add a splash of your favorite hot sauce.
- I make rectangular biscuits to eliminate the trimmings you get when the biscuits are cut into rounds. I find that when trimmings are rerolled, the second batch is never as good-looking as the first. But you can certainly cut out rounds of dough with a 3-inch biscuit cutter, gather up the scraps, and reroll until all the dough is cut out.
- Leftover biscuits freeze well in a resealable plastic bag. Let thaw overnight at room temperature, then reheat as desired.

Glazed Sweet Potatoes with Sesame and Chili

This is a sweet-and-savory side so rich you might want to pair it with a main course that's not sauced, like simple grilled pork chops or roast chicken. On the other hand, it could be the star of your Thanksgiving sides menu. It's easy to pull together, and the payoff is major.

Serves 4 to 6

1 tablespoon neutral cooking oil (such as avocado or canola)

3 (6-ounce) sweet potatoes, peeled and cut into ½-inch rounds

3 tablespoons soy sauce

2 tablespoons mirin or sweet white wine (such as Moscato or Riesling)

2 tablespoons light brown sugar

1 tablespoon toasted sesame oil

2 cloves garlic, minced

Gochugaru (Korean chili flakes), for serving

⅓ cup crumbled goat cheese (optional)

Sesame seeds, for serving

Heat the oil in a large skillet over medium-high heat. In batches, if needed, add the sweet potatoes and cook, stirring occasionally, until lightly browned all over, 5 to 7 minutes. (If you cooked in batches, return all of the sweet potatoes to the skillet.)

Whisk the soy sauce, mirin, brown sugar, sesame oil, and garlic with ½ cup water to dissolve the sugar. Pour over the sweet potatoes and bring to a boil. Reduce the heat to medium-low and cover tightly. Simmer, stirring occasionally, until the sweet potatoes are tender, about 20 minutes.

Uncover and increase the heat to high. Boil the liquid, stirring occasionally, until it is reduced to a glaze, about 5 minutes. Watch closely; you don't want the glaze to reduce too much and burn. Transfer to a serving dish, sprinkle with gochugaru, goat cheese (if using), and sesame seeds. Serve hot.

TAKEAWAY

- You'll most likely use standard, orange-fleshed sweet potatoes (yams) for this recipe. But the sauce is the dominant flavor, so you can use white- or yellow-fleshed Asian sweet potatoes (which aren't very sweet) or purple jewel yams.

Buttermilk Cornbread

There are two basic kinds of cornbread, sweet and not sweet. This one falls into the first category. It thinks it's a cake, and maybe you should lean into that. Warm it up and top with berries and whipped cream as a shortcake. Or go the opposite direction and top with Umami Chili (page 86).

Serves 8 to 12

1⅓ cups stone-ground yellow cornmeal

1¼ cups unbleached all-purpose flour

½ cup granulated sugar

1 tablespoon baking powder

1¼ teaspoons kosher salt

½ cup whole milk

½ cup buttermilk

½ cup neutral cooking oil (such as avocado or canola)

3 large eggs

Preheat the oven to 425°F. Lightly oil a 13x9x1-inch baking sheet (aka quarter-sheet pan; see Takeaways).

Whisk the cornmeal, flour, sugar, baking powder, and salt together in a medium bowl and make a well in the center. Whisk the milk, buttermilk, oil, and eggs together in another bowl, then pour into the well. Whisk just until combined. Spread evenly in the prepared pan.

Bake until the cornbread springs back when pressed in the center, 20 to 25 minutes. Let cool in the pan for 10 minutes. Cut into wedges and serve warm.

TAKEAWAYS

- Cornbread is a good canvas for other ingredients. Examples of add-ins include 1 cup shredded cheddar cheese, 2 tablespoons minced jalapeños, or ½ cup chopped pecans (or the Sweet and Spicy Walnuts on page 45 or the Candied Hazelnuts on page 240). Just fold your pick into the finished batter.
- A quarter-sheet pan (small baking sheet) is almost as useful in the kitchen as its big sibling, the half-sheet (large baking sheet), which is twice the size. The former is a good choice when roasting smaller amounts of food and will also fit in most toaster ovens.

Milk Bread Dinner Rolls

Milk bread is the lightest, fluffiest bread. This Japanese-style recipe uses *tangzhong*, a milk-and-flour roux that's incorporated into the dough, where the moistened gluten helps the bread rise. A lot. The rolls will stop the show at any meal, and the bun variation makes burgers the best ever. The dough is wet, so you need a stand mixer. This recipe makes hefty rolls, the way I like them, but I also give directions for a smaller size.

Serves 10

Tangzhong

¼ cup whole milk

2 tablespoons unbleached all-purpose flour

Dough

Scant ⅔ cup whole milk

2 large eggs plus 2 large egg yolks

3 tablespoons honey

2½ teaspoons instant yeast (one 2¼-ounce package)

3⅓ cups unbleached all-purpose flour

1½ teaspoons kosher salt

¾ cup (1½ sticks) unsalted butter, cut into tablespoons, at room temperature, plus more for the bowl and pan

1 large egg yolk beaten with 1 tablespoon heavy cream, for an egg wash

Flaky salt, for sprinkling

2 tablespoons unsalted butter, melted

Make the tangzhong: Mix the milk and 1 tablespoon water in a small saucepan. Add the flour and whisk until smooth. Bring to a boil over medium heat, stirring constantly with a wooden spoon, to make a thick roux. Scrape the roux into the bowl of a stand mixer.

Make the dough: Add the milk, eggs and yolks, honey, and yeast to the mixer bowl and whisk to combine. Add the flour and salt. Affix the bowl to the stand and fit with the paddle attachment. Mix on low speed until moistened, then increase the speed to medium and beat until the mixture mostly cleans the bowl's sides but sticks a bit to the bottom, about 2 minutes. With the mixer on, add the room-temperature butter, one tablespoon at a time, letting the dough absorb each addition before adding the next. When all the butter has been added, change to the dough hook. Knead on medium speed until the dough forms a slack ball that slaps around the bowl, about 2 minutes more.

Turn the dough out onto a lightly floured work surface. Working around the circumference of the dough, fold up the edges at the 12, 3, 6, and 9 o'clock positions and press them into the center to shape the dough into a taut ball. Turn the dough over so the folds are on the bottom. With your hands cupped on the sides of the ball, rotate the ball on the work surface a few times to shape it more. Place the dough in the bowl, smooth side up, and tightly cover with plastic wrap. Let the dough rise in a warm place until doubled in volume (if you poke your finger into the dough, the hole will fill in slowly), about 2 hours. (The dough can be refrigerated overnight.)

Lightly butter a large bowl. Turn out the dough onto an unfloured work surface. Lightly butter a 9-inch cake pan with 2-inch sides (or a 13x9-inch baking pan for smaller rolls). Divide the dough into ten equal pieces, about 3½ ounces each. (For smaller rolls, divide into 15 pieces, about 2⅓ ounces each.) One at a time, shape into a taut ball, using the technique in the previous step for forming the large ball of dough. Arrange the balls in the prepared pan, with two balls in the center and the remainder spaced around the circumference of the cake pan (or in rows in the bak-

(*recipe continues*)

ing pan). Cover loosely
with plastic wrap and let them rise until almost doubled in volume and touching, about 1½ hours (or about 2 hours if using chilled dough).

Preheat the oven to 400°F. Brush the tops of the balls with some of the egg wash. Sprinkle a pinch of flaky salt on each. Bake for 5 minutes. Reduce the oven temperature to 350°F. Continue baking until the rolls are golden brown and there is no sign of raw dough in the seams, 30 to 35 minutes (or about 20 minutes for the smaller rolls). (An instant-read thermometer inserted into a center roll should read about 200°F.)

Brush the tops of the baked dough with the melted butter. Let the rolls cool in the pan for 10 minutes. Remove from the pan, tear them apart, and serve warm or cooled.

Milk Bread Hamburger Buns:

Let the dough rise once. Line a large baking sheet with parchment paper. Divide the dough into ten equal pieces and shape each into a taut ball. Arrange well apart on the prepared pan and flatten slightly with your palm to about 3 inches in diameter. Loosely cover with plastic wrap and let rise in a warm place until almost doubled in volume, about 1¼ hours. Brush with the egg wash. Sprinkle with sesame seeds, if desired. Bake at 400°F for 5 minutes, then at 350°F until golden brown, about 10 minutes more. Brush with the melted butter, transfer to a wire cooling rack, and let cool completely.

TAKEAWAYS

- This dough is soft and moist with a tacky surface. It's not springy like a standard bread dough. Resist the temptation to add more flour. Because it has so much butter, don't let it rise where it is too warm (higher than 90°F) or the butter might leak out. The optimal temperature is about 80°F. If you have a proofing option in your oven, use it. Or place the dough in its container or pan in a microwave or standard oven with the door ajar. That will keep the utility light on to provide just the right amount of heat.

- Because the dough is so buttery, it doesn't stick to surfaces like other doughs and you won't need to flour the work surface. In fact, an unfloured surface will give you more traction for shaping the balls of dough.

- Your trusty kitchen scale is the best way to portion out the dough. Just weigh the entire batch (it will be around 1,000 g, allowing for variables), and divide that figure by the number of rolls you want to make. It should be about 100 g for larger rolls or hamburger buns, and 66 g for smaller rolls.

- Leftover dinner rolls freeze beautifully and are great to have on hand for breakfast sandwiches or to serve as a side dish.

Chapter 7

Sweets

Orange Chocoflan

Flan was my go-to dessert as a kid, right next to a nice piece of chocolate cake. This Frankensteins them, the custard mysteriously sinking into its own distinct layer. Be sure to chill the cake way ahead of serving (overnight is best) to set the beautiful flan.

Serves 8

Caramel

Neutral cooking oil (such as avocado or canola), for the pan

1 cup granulated sugar

Cake Batter

1 cup unbleached all-purpose flour

1 cup granulated sugar

½ cup natural cocoa powder (spooned into cup and leveled)

¾ teaspoon baking powder

½ teaspoon baking soda

¼ teaspoon kosher salt

¾ cup whole milk

1 large egg

2 tablespoons espresso or strong brewed coffee

1 teaspoon vanilla extract

Custard (Flan)

4 large eggs

1 (14-ounce) can condensed milk

1 (12-ounce) can evaporated milk

Finely grated zest of 1 orange

1 teaspoon vanilla extract

Make the caramel: Lightly coat the inside of a 9-inch square metal baking pan. Put the sugar in a medium saucepan, pour in ¼ cup water, and tilt the saucepan to moisten the sugar. Bring to a boil over high heat. Cover tightly and cook for 3 minutes. Uncover and cook without stirring, but occasionally swirling the saucepan by the handle, until the caramel is dark amber and smoking, 3 to 4 minutes. (Judge the caramel with your senses, not a timer.) Immediately pour into the prepared pan and tilt to evenly coat the bottom. Refrigerate the pan to cool and harden the caramel, about 10 minutes.

Make the cake batter: Preheat the oven to 350ºF. Whisk the flour, sugar, cocoa, baking powder, baking soda, and salt in a large bowl. Whisk the milk, egg, espresso, and vanilla in another bowl to combine. Pour into the flour mixture and whisk just until smooth. Scrape the batter into the caramel-coated pan.

Make the flan (custard): Whisk the eggs in a large bowl to break them up. Add the condensed milk, evaporated milk, orange zest, and vanilla and whisk to combine. Pour evenly over the batter. The custard will slowly sink to the bottom. Cover the dish with parchment paper and then a tightly sealed layer of aluminum foil.

Put a large roasting pan in the oven. Place the baking dish in the roasting pan and carefully pour enough hot tap water into the pan to come halfway up the sides of the dish. Bake until a wooden skewer inserted in the center of the top cake layer (through the parchment/foil top) comes out clean, 50 to 60 minutes.

Remove the dish from the pan, uncover, and let cool to room temperature. Cover with plastic wrap and refrigerate until chilled, at least 4 hours or preferably overnight.

To serve, uncover and run a dull knife inside the sides of the pan to loosen the cake. Return the cake pan to the roasting pan, add enough hot tap water to come about ½ inch up the sides, and let stand for about 5 minutes. (This will help melt the caramel.) Remove the pan from the hot water and dry the outside with a kitchen towel. Put a rimmed serving platter over the cake pan. Hold the pan and platter together, invert, and give them a shake to unmold the dessert. Remove the pan and scrape any caramel in the pan over the flan. Slice and serve chilled.

TAKEAWAYS

- Don't use Dutch-processed (alkalized) cocoa. It won't react with the baking soda to leaven the cake. Use a natural cocoa, such as Hershey's.
- Not into orange? Try banana (add ½ cup mashed ripe banana to the cake batter) or coffee (dissolve 2 teaspoons instant espresso powder in 2 teaspoons of hot water and add to the flan mixture).

Mexican Chocolate Tart

When it comes to the filling for this decadent tart, you can choose brandy, dark rum, or strong coffee as the top note. For me there is only one choice: coffee. It's the most Mexican thing to do, a little *cafesita* with dessert. This tart is a great way to showcase Mexican chocolate and its rustic, warm-spice mystique. My favorite brand is Abuelita, which feels like an appropriate nod to Grand and all grandmas who sneak us chocolate. But if you can't find it, I give you a workaround in the Takeaways.

Serves 8

Dough

1 cup unbleached all-purpose flour

3 tablespoons granulated sugar

¼ teaspoon kosher salt

6 tablespoons cold unsalted butter, cut into ½-inch cubes

1 large egg yolk

Filling

1 cup heavy cream

8 ounces Mexican chocolate (such as Abuelita; see Takeaways), coarsely chopped

2 tablespoons strong brewed coffee, brandy, or dark rum

2 large eggs

1 teaspoon vanilla extract

Whipped Cream

1 cup heavy cream

2 teaspoons granulated sugar

1 teaspoon vanilla extract

Caramel Sauce (page 238), for serving

Chocolate shavings (see Takeaways), for serving

To make the dough in a food processor: Pulse the flour, sugar, and salt in the processor to combine. Add the butter and pulse 10 to 15 times, until the mixture resembles coarse crumbs. In a small bowl, mix the yolk and 1 tablespoon cold water. With the machine running, pour the yolk mixture through the feed tube and process just until the dough is moistened. It will look crumbly but hold together when pressed between your thumb and forefinger. Remove the blade and gather and press the dough into a mass.

To make the dough by hand: Combine the flour, sugar, and salt in a medium bowl. Add the butter and cut it in with a pastry blender until the mixture resembles coarse crumbs. Mix the yolk and 1 tablespoon cold water and stir into the mixture to moisten. Gather and press the dough into a mass.

Crumble the dough into the tart pan and press it firmly and evenly into the bottom and up the sides so the dough stands about ⅛ inch above the edge of the pan. Prick the dough a few times with a fork. Freeze for 15 to 20 minutes.

Preheat the oven to 350°F. Line the dough with aluminum foil and fill with pie weights, dried beans, or raw rice (see Takeaways). Place the tart pan on a large baking sheet. Bake for 20 minutes, or until the tart dough looks set and is beginning to brown. Lift up and remove the foil with the weights and continue baking until the dough is golden brown, about 10 minutes more. Remove from the oven.

(*recipe continues*)

Make the filling: Heat the cream in a small saucepan over medium heat until simmering. Remove from the heat and add the chocolate and brandy. Let stand to soften the chocolate, about 2 minutes, then whisk until smooth. Whisk the eggs and vanilla in another medium bowl, then gradually whisk in the chocolate mixture. Pour into the warm tart shell. Return to the oven and bake (the filling will bubble) until the filling looks set, about 25 minutes. Don't worry if the filling cracks; the garnish can cover it up.

Transfer the tart to a wire cooling rack and let cool completely. (The tart can be covered with plastic wrap and refrigerated for up to 2 days.)

Make the whipped cream: In a chilled bowl, beat the cream, sugar, and vanilla with a handheld mixer at high speed until stiff peaks form.

Remove the sides of the pan. Slice the tart and serve chilled, with a dollop of whipped cream, a spoonful of caramel sauce, and a sprinkle of chocolate shavings.

TAKEAWAYS

- If you do a lot of baking, aluminum or ceramic pie weights are a good investment. However, you can easily substitute about 2 cups dried raw rice or beans. You can reuse these a few times, but when they start to smell funky, throw them out and start with a fresh batch. For this reason, buying dedicated weights may be a good investment.

- Mexican chocolate is sweeter and coarser than the typical chocolate bar. It's mainly used for making beverages and sauces. Abuelita (*little grandma* in Spanish) is a popular brand sold in a box with 3.1-ounce tablets, which are typically crushed and melted in warmed milk to make hot chocolate. While I hope you have a kitchen scale, if you need to eyeball the 8 ounces in this recipe, it's about 2¾ tablets.

- For this recipe, a substitute for the Mexican chocolate would be 8 ounces semisweet chocolate (about 55 percent cacao content) plus 2 tablespoons sugar and ¼ teaspoon ground cinnamon.

- To make chocolate shavings, use a chunk of Mexican, semisweet, or bittersweet chocolate (at least 2 ounces, large enough for you to get a good grip on it). Microwave it on high for a few seconds to just warm the surface—don't melt it. Over a sheet of parchment or waxed paper, press hard on the chocolate with a swivel vegetable peeler, shaving off shards and letting them fall on the paper. Try not to melt the shavings with your fingers.

& ALL THE
PROOF

Pumpkin Mousse Pie with Gingersnap Crust

I loved pumpkin so much from an early age that Grand called me Pumpkin. All those empanadas and pies imprinted themselves on my palate. So don't give me your shade for pumpkin spice. I get it. That latte has eaten our culture. But comfort yourself with the fact that it's basically chai, just a beautiful spice blend that shines in this silky pie. It belongs on your Thanksgiving menu, all the better because it takes minimal baking and there's never enough room in the oven.

Serves 8

Pie Shell

2½ cups (roughly one 14-ounce box) finely crushed gingersnap cookies (use a food processor)

½ cup packed light brown sugar

10 tablespoons (1¼ sticks) unsalted butter

Mousse Filling

9 ounces mascarpone

9 ounces creamy, rindless goat cheese

1 cup canned pumpkin

½ cup packed light brown sugar

1 tablespoon plus ½ teaspoon pumpkin pie spice (see Takeaways)

1 teaspoon vanilla extract

2 tablespoons finely chopped pistachios, for garnish

Make the pie shell: Preheat the oven to 350°F. Mix the cookie crumbs, sugar, and melted butter in a medium bowl until the crumbs are moistened. Press firmly and evenly into the bottom and up the sides of a 9-inch pie pan. Bake on a large baking sheet until the crust smells toasty, about 10 minutes. Cool completely.

Make the mousse: Beat the mascarpone, goat cheese, pumpkin, brown sugar, pumpkin pie spice, and vanilla together in a medium bowl with an electric mixer on medium speed until thoroughly combined. Spread the filling in the cooled crust. Refrigerate uncovered until the filling is chilled and set, at least 1 hour. If chilling longer (more than 2 hours or up to 2 days), cover loosely with plastic wrap and tent it with toothpicks if you're worried about messing up the glossy surface.

Sprinkle the pistachios over the filling, slice, and serve on dessert plates.

TAKEAWAYS

- You can buy pumpkin pie spice, but I make my own, as I have all the spices on hand anyway. Mix 1 teaspoon ground cinnamon, 1 teaspoon ground ginger, ½ teaspoon ground allspice, ½ teaspoon freshly grated nutmeg, ¼ teaspoon ground cardamom (preferably freshly ground seeds from green cardamom pods), and ¼ teaspoon ground cloves. If you buy pumpkin pie spice, add ground cardamom to give it that chai note, as most brands won't include it.

- Use freshly roasted pumpkin puree, if you're feeling ambitious. Pie pumpkin, acorn squash, or butternut squash all work well for roasting and pureeing. About 1¼ pounds raw squash yields 1 cup puree. Preheat the oven to 400°F. Rinse and dry the pumpkin, then halve and deseed it. Place the pumpkin cut-side down on a parchment-lined baking sheet and roast until fork-tender, 35 to 45 minutes. Let cool, then use a large metal spoon to scoop the flesh into a heavy-duty blender, discarding the peel. Puree the pumpkin, adding 1 tablespoon water at a time until smooth. (The puree can be refrigerated in a covered container for up to 3 days or frozen for up to 3 months.)

Mango Sherbet with Chamoy

The way I say mango (like *mongo*) is a thing online. Commenters love to heckle. But everybody back home says it like I do, with the tongue low and flat for the back vowel. Some of these same people were with me in middle school, when we'd walk over to this old lady's house and buy *mangonada* for a quarter. It was a clear Solo cup with frozen fruit on a stick coated in chamoy and Tajín. This sherbet is an attempt to put that essence of my childhood in a bowl.

Serves 6 to 8

6 ripe mangoes (about 2½ pounds)

1 (14-ounce) can sweetened condensed milk

⅓ cup plus 1 tablespoon maple syrup or dark agave syrup

About ½ cup Homemade Chamoy (page 236) or store-bought, for serving

Piment d'Espelette or Tajín, for serving

Put a metal 9x5-inch loaf pan in the freezer to chill for 30 to 60 minutes.

Pit, peel, and coarsely chop the mangoes. Process the mangoes, condensed milk, and maple syrup in a food processor or heavy-duty blender until pureed, scraping down the sides of the jar as needed. Pour into the cold pan and cover with plastic wrap, pressing the wrap directly onto the puree. Freeze until solid, at least 6 hours or overnight. (The sherbet will freeze hard if frozen overnight. It is easiest to scoop when it's frozen but still somewhat soft, after 6 to 8 hours. If the sherbet is hardened, let it thaw at room temperature for a few minutes before serving.)

Scoop the sherbet into bowls. Top each serving with a drizzle of chamoy and a sprinkle of piment d'Espelette. Serve immediately.

TAKEAWAYS

- If you were to simply freeze the plain mango puree, it would get icy and not be very good to eat. The condensed milk and maple syrup work together to keep the ice crystals from getting too big so the texture stays smooth.
- Chilling the metal loaf pan before adding the sherbet also helps with texture, because the faster it freezes the smaller the ice crystals. Give the pan a good stretch in the freezer if you can, but no less than 30 minutes.
- Piment d'Espelette is a mild Basque chile with a soft fruitiness. It looks a little nicer than Tajín, the OG Mexican seasoning powder of dried chiles and lime. You pick.

Balsamic Berry Slab Pie

Making pie this way is about two things. 1) I'd rather use a baking sheet than a round tin because you get more pie. 2) Who doesn't want pie in slabs? This is perfect for a party because of the size and unspoken invitation to get in there. But before you dive into making it, here are some fundamentals I learned watching pastry chefs work: A stovetop berry filling is often preferable to a raw one, because the flavor really comes through without any extra thickener. Balsamic vinegar isn't just a great flavoring for the berries; it helps to gel the juices. Make the filling a day ahead so it has time to cool and set. That last one is crucial.

Serves 9 or 12

Filling

3 cups fresh strawberries (1 pound), hulled and halved (see Takeaways)

2 cups (1 dry pint) fresh blueberries

1⅓ cups fresh blackberries

1⅓ cups fresh raspberries

1 cup maple sugar or packed light brown sugar

2 tablespoons aged balsamic vinegar

Flaky Pastry Dough (page 241), divided into 2 portions, one slightly larger than the other

Egg wash: 1 large egg yolk mixed with 2 teaspoons whole milk

Make the filling: Put a saucer in the freezer to chill. Mix all the berries, the maple sugar, and vinegar together in a large, heavy nonreactive saucepan and let stand until the berries give off some juices, about 15 minutes. Bring to a simmer over medium heat, stirring often to avoid scorching, until the juices are thickened, 35 to 40 minutes. To check for thickness, put about a teaspoon of the juice on the chilled saucer—if you can drag your finger through the juices to cut a clean swath, it's ready (see Takeaways for details). You should have about 1 quart cooked filling. Transfer to a bowl and let cool. Cover and refrigerate overnight until chilled and set.

On a lightly floured work surface, roll out the larger portion of the dough into a 16x12-inch rectangle about ⅛-inch thick. Fit into a 13x9-inch baking sheet (quarter-sheet pan), letting the excess hang over the sides and fitting it tightly into the corners. Fold the dough over at the rim of the pan and press the dough against the sides so it stands about ¼ inch above the edge. Spread the chilled filling in the pan. Put the pie in the freezer to keep cold while cutting the strips.

(*recipe continues*)

TAKEAWAYS

- This berry filling is actually a jam. To check the thickness, I use the chilled saucer test, which has been around forever. If the filling is loose and unset when you run a finger through it on that cold plate, boil it for a few minutes more, and test again (refreezing the saucer in the interim).
- Supermarket balsamic vinegar is thin and sharp, and while it will work in the filling, aged balsamic vinegar (found in specialty markets) is much richer and thicker. Any aged balsamic works—no need to use a 25-year bottle.
- Any combination of berries (or even one kind) adding up to about 8 cups will do here. Just don't use all strawberries, because they lose flavor and color when baked and should be combined with other berries.
- Use a dark sugar (maple or light brown) to deepen the color of the filling.
- Many pie dough recipes gather the dough into a ball for chilling. But if you're going to roll the dough into a rectangle to fit the pan, it makes sense to mold it into that shape for its chill.
- Check the size of the baking sheet to be sure it is truly 9x13 inches (i.e., a quarter-sheet pan). Some brands are larger, more like 10x14 inches.
- To double the recipe, use a half-sheet pan (18x13-inch). You can increase both the dough and filling by half or roll the dough thinner and spread the filling shallower for a crispy jam bar. For this second method, start checking for doneness around 35 minutes, since the crust will brown faster.

Roll out the remaining smaller disc of dough to a 13x9-inch rectangle. Using a sharp knife or a pizza wheel, cut the long way into six strips about 13 inches long and 1½ inches wide. Weave (or simply crisscross) the strips in a diagonal pattern over the filling. Fold the overhanging dough in to cover the edges of the strips. Chill the pie in the freezer for about 15 minutes.

Meanwhile, preheat the oven to 375ºF. Line a large baking sheet with parchment paper (to help with cleanup if the filling boils over). Lightly brush the dough with the egg wash. Place the pie on the lined pan and bake until the crust is golden brown, about 45 minutes. Let cool completely on a wire cooling rack.
Cut into nine or twelve rectangles and serve. (The pie can be covered with plastic wrap and stored at room temperature for up to 2 days.)

Chai Flan

Chai spices bring an unexpected flavor to my family favorite in this gorgeous dessert that absolutely tastes as good as it looks. But only make flan when you're willing to let it chill for a few hours or even overnight—it cannot be rushed. Try to unmold it before it's time and you'll end up with un-gorgeous mush.

Serves 8

1 cup granulated sugar

1 (14-ounce) can sweetened condensed milk

1¾ cups whole milk

1 teaspoon ground ginger

½ teaspoon black peppercorns

½ teaspoon allspice berries

½ teaspoon fennel seeds

⅛ teaspoon ground turmeric

3 green cardamom pods, crushed

1 star anise, broken into points

1 (3-inch) stick cinnamon

2 whole cloves

1 tablespoon loose leaf black tea (such as English Breakfast), or 3 tea bags

4 large eggs

Make the caramel: Put the sugar in a medium saucepan and pour in ¼ cup water. Bring to a boil over high heat. Cover tightly and cook for 3 minutes. Uncover and cook, without stirring but occasionally swirling the saucepan by the handle, until the caramel is dark amber and smoking, 4 to 5 minutes. (Judge the caramel with your senses, not with a timer.) Immediately pour the caramel in a 9½-inch deep-dish pie plate and tilt the plate to evenly coat the bottom. Let the caramel cool and harden while making the custard.

Position a rack in the center of the oven and preheat to 350°F. In a medium saucepan, whisk the condensed milk, whole milk, ginger, peppercorns, allspice, fennel, turmeric, cardamom, star anise, cinnamon, and cloves to combine. Bring to a simmer over medium heat. Remove from the heat, stir in the tea, and infuse for 3 minutes. Strain the spiced milk through a wire mesh sieve into a 1-quart measuring cup or bowl with a spout and press hard on the solids. Discard the solids.

Whisk the eggs in a large bowl. Gradually whisk in the spiced milk until well blended. Strain through a wire mesh sieve into the caramel-coated pie plate. Cover the pie plate with parchment paper and add a tightly sealed layer of aluminum foil. Put a large roasting pan in the oven. Place the pie plate in the roasting pan and add enough hot water to the pan to come halfway up the sides of the pie plate. Bake until the flan is set and jiggles as a unit when the dish is shaken, about 55 minutes. (You'll have to remove the roasting pan setup from the oven to open the covering and check.) Carefully remove the plate from the pan with the hot water. Remove the foil and let the flan cool on a wire cooling rack until tepid, about 1 hour.

Cover the flan with plastic wrap and refrigerate until chilled, at least 4 hours or up to 3 days. Uncover the flan and run a dinner knife around the inside of the pie plate to release the flan. Place a serving dish with a lip (to contain the caramel) over the flan and invert them together, then unmold the flan. Cut into wedges and serve on dessert dishes, spooning some caramel over each.

TAKEAWAYS

- Be careful when adding the hot spiced milk to the eggs. The pour should be gradual to temper the eggs. If you add it all at once, you could get scrambled eggs instead of custard.

- The flan will not set up completely until it's chilled. So even if it looks wobbly out of the oven, have faith. Let it cool, let it chill, and you chill, too.

Arroz con Leche

My ma knew how to use leftovers, her best spinoff from dinner being rice pudding. All you need is old rice, condensed milk, and a couple accents. Garnish with your favorite fresh fruit, whether mango slices, berries, peaches, papaya—it's all good. And so is the Caramel Sauce on page 238. I serve this dessert with bananas that have been sugared and caramelized because they cover both those bases and bring some crunch, though you could also add texture with chopped nuts.

Serves 6 to 8

1 (14-ounce) can sweetened condensed milk

½ cup heavy cream

¼ cup maple sugar or granulated sugar

1 teaspoon ground cinnamon

4 cups cooked white rice (any variety; see Takeaway)

2 large eggs

1 teaspoon vanilla extract

2 to 3 ripe bananas, peeled and cut into 18 to 24 rounds

½ cup granulated sugar, for the bananas

Flaky salt

Whisk the condensed milk, cream, maple sugar, and cinnamon together in a medium saucepan. Add the rice and stir to combine. Cook over medium heat, stirring often, until simmering.

Beat the eggs in a heatproof medium bowl. Beat in about 1 cup of the hot rice mixture. Stir the mixture back into the saucepan and cook, stirring constantly, until lightly thickened and the pudding reads 185ºF on an instant-read thermometer. Remove from the heat and stir in the vanilla. Divide among six to eight serving bowls and let cool until tepid, about 30 minutes. Cover and refrigerate until chilled, at least 1 hour or overnight.

Arrange the banana rounds on a broiler pan and sprinkle with the granulated sugar. Using a kitchen torch, wave the flame closely over the sugar until it caramelizes. (Or position a broiler rack 3 inches from the source of heat and preheat on high. Line a broiler pan with aluminum foil, arrange the banana rounds on the foil, and sprinkle with the granulated sugar. Broil, watching carefully so the bananas don't burn, until the sugar caramelizes, about 1 minute.)

With a metal spatula, top each chilled serving with three banana rounds, sprinkle with flaky salt, and serve.

TAKEAWAY

- You can use any kind of plain cooked white rice—long-grain, basmati, jasmine, sushi, even brown—because the pudding makes all of it taste good.

Forbidden Black Rice Marshmallow Bars

We love crispy stuff in a brick of buttery marshmallow. My spin swaps the classic rice cereal for forbidden black rice, bringing a little nutty flavor and a lot of crunch. The grains take a dip in hot oil, puff up like tiny popcorn, and come out speckled black—which looks rad against the marshmallow's stark white. The puffed rice is tasty on its own, just sprinkled with kosher salt while still warm. Use it as a textural note (see Takeaways), or put that snack right in your face.

Makes 1 dozen

Rice or peanut oil, for deep-frying and oiling the pan and utensils

Generous 2 cups forbidden black rice (see Takeaways)

3 tablespoons unsalted butter

1 (10-ounce) package miniature marshmallows

Flaky salt, for topping

Line a large baking sheet with two layers of paper towels. Pour enough oil into a large saucepan to come about halfway up the sides. Heat over high heat until it registers 375°F on an instant-read thermometer (and make sure to bring the oil back up to temp between batches). In three or four batches, carefully add the rice and fry until it rises to the surface and is puffed, about 10 seconds. (It won't look as puffed as rice breakfast cereal.) Using a heatproof wire mesh sieve or skimmer, transfer the rice to the paper towels. Cover with another double layer of paper towels and pat to absorb more oil. Cool completely. You should have about 5 cups puffed rice.

Lightly oil an 8-inch square baking pan, a large silicone spatula, and a thin knife. Melt the butter in a large saucepan over medium-low heat. Add the marshmallows and heat, stirring often to avoid scorching on the bottom of the pan, until melted and smooth, about 3 minutes. Remove from the heat, add the puffed rice, and stir well. Using the oiled spatula, evenly spread and press the mixture in the pan. Let cool for a few minutes. Using the oiled knife, score the marshmallow mixture into twelve equal rectangles. Add a pinch of flaky salt to the top of each bar and press gently to adhere. Let cool completely.

Using an oiled knife, cut through the scoring to create twelve bars and remove from the pan. (The bars can be stored in an airtight container, layers separated with parchment paper, at room temperature for up to 5 days.)

TAKEAWAYS

- Use only forbidden black rice for this—any old black rice won't work. The real deal is sold at well-stocked Asian markets and online.
- Try the puffed grains as a topping on yogurt, creamy soups, simple salads, stir-fries, and sushi rolls. Anywhere you want a bit of crunch and color.

Big Cinnamon Buns with Cream Cheese Icing

When cinnamon rolls grow up, they turn into buns girthy enough to handle my chili (page 86). There are no surprises with the ingredients here, because you want to taste cinnamon, butter, vanilla, and all the baked-in love.

Serves 8

Dough

5 cups unbleached all-purpose flour, plus more for rolling

1 cup whole milk, lukewarm (heat in a microwave to take off the chill)

4½ teaspoons instant yeast (two ¼-ounce packages)

½ cup plus ¼ teaspoon granulated sugar

2 teaspoons kosher salt

5 tablespoons unsalted butter, plus additional softened butter for the bowl and pan

3 large eggs

1 teaspoon vanilla extract

Filling

½ cup packed light brown sugar

½ cup (1 stick) unsalted butter, at room temperature

2 teaspoons ground cinnamon (preferably Ceylon or Saigon)

Cream Cheese Icing

2 ounces cream cheese, at room temperature

2 tablespoons unsalted butter, at room temperature

1½ cups powdered sugar

1 tablespoon whole milk, or more as needed

1 teaspoon fresh lemon juice

1 teaspoon vanilla extract

2 tablespoons unsalted butter, melted, for brushing

Make a sponge: Using a silicone spatula, stir ½ cup of the flour, ½ cup of the milk, 1 teaspoon of the yeast, and the ¼ teaspoon sugar together in a small bowl until smooth. Scrape down the sides of the bowl, cover with plastic wrap, and let stand in a warm place until the sponge looks bubbly, about 30 minutes.

To make the dough in a stand mixer: Whisk the remaining 4½ cups flour, 3½ teaspoons yeast, ½ cup sugar, and the salt in the bowl of a stand mixer to combine. Melt the butter in a medium saucepan over medium heat. Remove from the heat and add the remaining ½ cup milk. Pour into a medium bowl and let cool, stirring often, until tepid, about 5 minutes. Add the sponge, eggs, and vanilla and whisk until the sponge breaks up. Add to the flour mixture in the mixer bowl, affix the bowl to the mixer, and mix with the paddle attachment on low speed until the dough comes together. Switch to the dough hook and knead on medium-low speed, pulling down the dough when it climbs up the hook. Continue until the dough is smooth and elastic, but still tacky, and passes the windowpane test (see Takeaways), about 6 minutes. Do not add more flour unless the dough is very wet and sticky.

To make the dough by hand: Stir the remaining flour, yeast, and sugar with the salt in a large bowl and make a well in the center. In a medium bowl, mix the remaining milk with the melted butter and beat in the eggs and vanilla. Stir into the sponge and mix to combine. Pour into the well and stir to make a stiff, shaggy dough. Turn out onto a lightly floured work surface and knead, adding sprinkles of flour as necessary, until smooth and elastic, but still tacky, about 8 minutes. Keep the dough on the soft side and don't add too much flour.

Lightly butter a large bowl. Form the dough into a ball, transfer to the bowl, turn to coat, and leave smooth side up. Cover tightly with plastic wrap and let stand in a warm place until puffy, about 1½ hours.

Make the filling: Beat the brown sugar, softened butter, and cinnamon in the bowl of a stand mixer fitted with the paddle attachment until smooth. Or mix in a medium bowl with a hand mixer set at medium speed.

(*recipe continues*)

Form the rolls: Lightly butter a 9x13-inch baking pan. Punch down the dough and transfer to a lightly floured work surface. Pat the dough into a rough rectangle. Dust the top with flour. Roll out into a 16x14-inch rectangle, with the long side facing you. Stretch and shape the corners into right angles.

Spread the filling over the dough (an offset spatula works well), leaving a 1-inch border, and moisten the top border with a little water. Starting at a long side, roll up the dough into a cylinder and pinch the long seam closed.

Using a sharp thin knife, cut the dough crosswise into eight 2-inch-thick rolls. Arrange the rolls, spaced equally apart, in the pan. Gently press on the tops of the rolls to widen them slightly. Cover loosely with plastic wrap and let stand in a warm place until the rolls look puffy, about 1¼ hours. (Or refrigerate for up to 16 hours.)

Preheat the oven to 350ºF. Uncover the rolls and bake until golden brown (an instant-read thermometer inserted in the center of the rolls will read over 190ºF), about 30 minutes. (If the centers of the rolls have risen into peaks, just push them down.) Brush melted butter over the tops of the buns. Let cool in the pan for 15 minutes.

Make the icing: Heat the cream cheese and butter in a medium saucepan over medium heat until they begin to melt. Add the powdered sugar, milk, lemon juice, and vanilla and whisk until the mixture is smooth and warm, adding more milk a teaspoon at a time if it's too thick to pour easily. Pour the icing over the warm rolls. Let cool for 15 minutes, or cool completely. Remove the buns from the pan and serve warm or at room temp. (The buns are best the day they are made. Leftover buns can be wrapped in aluminum foil and stored at room temperature for up to 2 days. Reheat individual buns in a microwave oven for 30 seconds on high power.)

TAKEAWAYS

- Take the butter and cream cheese for the icing out of your fridge as soon as you start making the dough so they're good and soft when you need them.
- Active dry yeast is a pain in the ass. Use instant yeast (also called rapid-rise or bread-machine yeast). It dissolves readily in a dough, instead of needing to be dissolved first in liquid at a specific temp. And it's way less temperamental, so the temperature of the milk for the sponge isn't something to sweat. The milk should just feel lukewarm to the touch, and you can warm it in the saucepan you'll use for melting the butter.
- The windowpane test is how you tell if you've kneaded enough gluten into the bread. Pinch off a small piece of dough and gently stretch it between your fingers. If you can pull it thin enough to see light through it without the dough tearing, it's ready. If it rips, keep kneading.

Hazelnut Coffee Soda

Anyone who knows me knows the grip coffee has on my heart. Not just any coffee, but Espresso Vivace, my all-time favorite Seattle coffee roaster and shop. This sipping dessert was inspired by their Cafe Nico drink: coffee with touches of orange and vanilla syrups, cinnamon, and a hit of steamed cream, finished with fragrant orange peel. I used to make the drink for everybody at work, and I love channeling Cafe Nico in this hazelnut soda. I like to pull fresh espresso, but I've made it with the instant kind, as well as dark roast from a moka coffee pot. If you really want to hammer home the idea of dessert, add that scoop of ice cream.

Serves 2

⅓ cup heavy cream

1 tablespoon powdered sugar

¼ teaspoon vanilla extract

Finely grated zest of ½ orange, plus 2 strips orange zest (removed with a vegetable peeler) for garnish

4 tablespoons cooled brewed espresso

4 tablespoons Hazelnut Syrup plus 4 tablespoons finely chopped Candied Hazelnuts (page 240)

Cinnamon (preferably Ceylon or Saigon)

Chilled club soda, as needed

2 large scoops vanilla or coffee ice cream (optional)

Whip the cream, powdered sugar, vanilla, and grated orange zest in a small chilled bowl with an electric mixer set on high until stiff. Cover and refrigerate until ready to use (within 8 hours for best texture).

For each serving, stir 2 tablespoons espresso and 2 tablespoons syrup in a tall glass, then dust with cinnamon. Add ice and top off with enough club soda to come about 1 inch from the top of the glass. Perch a scoop of ice cream on the lip of the glass if you like. Add a big dollop of the whipped cream, sprinkle with 2 tablespoons candied hazelnuts, and garnish with an orange zest strip. Serve immediately with a long iced-tea spoon and a straw.

TAKEAWAY

- By whipping the orange zest with the cream from the beginning, you'll agitate the zest to knock out more citrus oil and flavor. So don't stir it in at the end.

Chapter 8

Pantry

Chicken Stock (aka Chicken Jell-O)

Make your own stock. Yeah, I know you can buy cans of chicken broth. But the difference between homemade and canned is huge. Because "broth" isn't necessarily made with bones, and bones are where the magic is. Gelatin and collagen cook out to give stock body and a mouthfeel you won't get out of a can, not to mention bonus nutrition. I call it chicken Jell-O, because it sets up and jiggles after a night in the fridge. It also turns scraps into gold. Anytime you have chicken trimmings/bones, carrot peels, onion butts, and celery ends, stash them in a gallon freezer bag and freeze. When it's full, you're ready to cook it down (you don't even have to thaw it out first). But if you haven't built up that supply, try this recipe.

Makes about 3 quarts

3 to 4 pounds chicken wings, cut between the joints; or chicken backs, hacked into chunks with a large knife or cleaver

1 medium yellow onion, with skin, coarsely chopped (or 1 cup coarsely chopped scallions and/or leeks, white and pale green parts only)

1 medium carrot, coarsely chopped

1 medium celery rib, coarsely chopped

4 sprigs fresh parsley

4 sprigs fresh thyme or ½ teaspoon dried thyme

2 bay leaves

1 teaspoon black peppercorns

Put the chicken into a tall pot and add enough cold water to cover by about 2 inches. Bring to a boil over high heat and skim off the white scum on the surface. (This is just coagulated proteins from the bones, which are harmless but will cloud the stock.) Add the onion, carrot, celery, parsley, thyme, bay leaves, and peppercorns and return to the boil. Reduce the heat to medium-low and cook at a brisk simmer (not a boil) until the liquid reduces by half, 6 to 8 hours.

Strain the stock through a wire sieve into a larger bowl and let stand until cooled. Transfer to covered containers and refrigerate for up to 3 days, or freeze for up to 3 months.

Turkey Stock:

Substitute turkey wings, cut between the joints, for the chicken wings. If you have a cleaver, chop the turkey wing parts in half again through the bone.

TAKEAWAYS

- Allow lots of time for this. It's a great rainy-day project, and your kitchen will smell amazing. I sometimes let my stock cook overnight. If you want to try making it in an instant pressure cooker, go ahead—but most pots will only hold about half the ingredients. Follow the directions for your pot's maximum capacity.
- Don't salt your stock. Salt will be an ingredient in whatever recipe uses the stock, so keep it plain.
- Because the chicken cooks for so long, the drained meat doesn't have much flavor or nutrition left. You could use it to bulk up pet food, but there's not much else you can do with it.

Vegetable Stock

Vegetable stock is quick to make, and it's a good alternative when you want a flavorful liquid but are out of chicken stock (or are cooking vegetarian). You could add other veggies and their trimmings, either root veg (like parsnips) or members of the onion family (like leeks). Make a batch to freeze so it's ready when you are.

Makes about 1½ quarts

2 tablespoons neutral cooking oil (such as avocado or canola)

1 medium yellow onion, chopped

2 medium carrots, chopped

2 medium celery ribs, chopped

6 to 8 white, button, or cremini mushrooms (or any mushroom trimmings), chopped

4 sprigs fresh parsley

¼ teaspoon dried thyme, or 4 sprigs fresh thyme

1 teaspoon kosher salt

5 black peppercorns

1 bay leaf

Heat the oil in a large saucepan over medium heat. Add the onion, carrots, celery, and mushrooms and cover. Cook, stirring occasionally, until the onions are tender, about 4 minutes. Stir in 2 quarts cold water and the parsley, thyme, salt, peppercorns, and bay leaf. Bring to a boil over high heat.

Reduce the heat to low and simmer, uncovered, until the stock is full-flavored, about 45 minutes. Strain through a wire sieve into a large bowl, discarding the solids. (The stock can be cooled, covered, and refrigerated for up to 5 days or frozen for up to 3 months.)

Homemade Chorizo

I use premade chorizo plenty. Usually the fresh, soft stuff you find in a tube at Mexican markets, ready to squeeze into a pan of frying potatoes and eggs. This and the smoked Spanish sausages (which are hard and sliceable) are getting more common at supermarkets, too. That said, soft chorizo is easy to make at home and customize with the spices. Use it in the Concha Breakfast Sandwiches (page 143) and Queso Flameado (page 37).

Serves 4

3 tablespoons sweet paprika

1½ teaspoons kosher salt

1 teaspoon ground guajillo chile or chili powder

½ teaspoon dried oregano

½ teaspoon freshly ground black pepper

½ teaspoon onion powder

½ teaspoon garlic powder

½ teaspoon ground cumin

½ teaspoon citric acid (sour salt)

Pinch of ground cinnamon

1 pound ground pork

4 ounces frozen lard, shredded on the large holes of a box grater (optional; see Takeaway)

½ cup unseasoned rice vinegar, chilled

Whisk the paprika, salt, ground guajillo, oregano, pepper, onion powder, garlic powder, cumin, citric acid, and cinnamon in a small bowl to combine well.

Put the pork, frozen lard, if using, and rice vinegar in a medium bowl. Add the spice mixture and mix well with your hands. If you're using the chorizo for sandwiches, form into 4 patties, about ¾-inch thick. Cover and refrigerate until ready to use, up to 24 hours (or freeze for up to 3 months).

TAKEAWAY

- Working lard into the raw meat might not sound appetizing, but it makes the cooked meat silkier and juicier. So, why is it optional? 1) Most ground pork doesn't need additional fat (especially the higher-fat blends Asian markets tend to sell). 2) Not everyone has frozen lard on hand. 3) Maybe you want a healthier option. Using lard will give you better texture and a more authentic result, but your chorizo will succeed without it.

Pickled Red Peppers

Pepper season is the time to make your own pickled ones. And you should make tons, because it's a key condiment to have around. Mine go on everything, from pizza to steak. I use red bells here, but if you like it spicier, use a hotter pepper like cherry, Fresno, or the Hungarian kind, which are found in my favorite jarred local brand, Mama Lil's.

Makes about 1 quart

3 large red bell peppers

2 cups extra virgin olive oil

2 tablespoons dried oregano

2 teaspoons kosher salt

½ teaspoon coarsely ground black pepper

¼ teaspoon crushed hot red pepper

½ cup red wine vinegar

Cut the peppers into pieces about 2 inches long and 1 inch wide and discard the stems, seeds, and ribs. Put the peppers in a nonreactive skillet and add the oil, oregano, salt, black pepper, and red pepper. The oil will only partially cover the peppers, but the peppers will shrink. Bring to a boil over high heat. Reduce the heat to medium-low and simmer, stirring occasionally, until the peppers are tender, about 30 minutes. Do not rush this step. Remove from the heat.

Using a slotted spoon, transfer the bell peppers to a 1-quart storage container, such as a canning jar, and pour in the vinegar. Ladle enough of the seasoned oil into the container to cover the peppers. (Reserve the remaining oil; see Takeaway.) Let cool to room temperature.

Cover tightly and refrigerate for 1 day before using. (The peppers can be refrigerated for up to 1 month.) Let stand at room temperature to liquefy the chilled oil before using, about 30 minutes.

TAKEAWAY

- If you have more oil than you need for covering the peppers in the last step, leftovers can be transferred to a covered container, cooled, and refrigerated for up to 2 weeks (it's vital to refrigerate the herbed oil). With some red wine vinegar, it makes a great Italian salad dressing.

Orange-Pickled Red Onions

Pickling really brings out the pinkness of red onion. It's a pretty accent that also adds bright flavor to everything—tacos and nachos, eggs and fried rice, burgers and salads. So I like always having a container on hand. The pickling liquid here is more of a flavoring than a preservative, so be sure to store the onions in the fridge.

Makes about 1 quart

1 large red onion, cut into thin half-moons

1½ teaspoons cumin seeds

2 cups unseasoned rice vinegar

Zest of ½ navel orange, removed in strips with a vegetable peeler

⅓ cup fresh orange juice

½ fresh jalapeño chile, cut into thin rounds, with seeds

4 teaspoons kosher salt

1 teaspoon gochugaru (Korean chili flakes)

Pack the onion in a heatproof 1-quart container with a lid.

Heat a small saucepan over medium-high heat. Add the cumin seeds and cook, stirring occasionally, until fragrant and toasted, about 1 minute. Add 1 cup water, the vinegar, orange zest strips, orange juice, jalapeño, salt, and gochugaru and bring to a boil. Pour the liquid over the onions and let cool. Cover and refrigerate overnight before using. (The onions can be refrigerated in the container for up to 1 month.)

Banh Mi Pickles

While these crisp pickles are meant as a component of the Nashville Chicken Banh Mi on page 139, they're so tasty you'll find homes for them far outside that sandwich. And they're quick—ready to munch as soon as they cool in the brine.

Makes about 1 quart

1 medium carrot, cut into thin strips

1 Kirby cucumber, scrubbed (but unpeeled) and cut into thin strips

½ small red onion, cut into thin half-moons

1½ cups rice wine vinegar

¼ cup granulated sugar

1 clove garlic, crushed under a knife and peeled

1 tablespoon kosher salt

¼ teaspoon yellow mustard seeds

¼ teaspoon celery seed

6 black peppercorns

1 whole clove

Pinch of ground turmeric

Put the carrot, cucumber, and red onion in a 1-quart container. Bring the vinegar, sugar, garlic, salt, mustard seeds, celery seed, peppercorns, clove, and turmeric to a boil in a small nonreactive saucepan over high heat. Strain over the vegetables and discard the spices. Let stand until cooled. (The pickles can be covered and refrigerated for up to 1 month.) Drain before using.

Roasted Salsa Verde

There's something so satisfying about roasting the fuck out of a pan of vegetables to make this salsa. I take them all the way to almost burned because I want serious smoky flavor in there. I use two chiles every time, but you can try just one until you establish your own heat level. You can always add more spice, but you can't take it out.

Makes about 3 cups

1½ pounds tomatillos, husked and rinsed to remove any sticky residue

1 medium yellow onion, cut into thick half-moons

10 cloves garlic, peeled

1 jalapeño chile, halved lengthwise, with seeds

1 serrano chile, halved lengthwise, with seeds (optional)

2 tablespoons duck fat or olive oil

Kosher salt

½ cup packed fresh cilantro leaves and thin stems

2 tablespoons fresh lime juice

Position a rack in the center of the oven and preheat to 500°F. Put the tomatillos, onion, garlic, jalapeño, and serrano (if using) on a large baking sheet. Toss with the duck fat and 1 teaspoon salt.

Roast, stirring occasionally (the vegetables on the ends will brown first), until the ingredients are well charred and the tomatillos are bursting, 15 to 20 minutes. Let cool slightly.

Transfer to a heavy-duty blender (or a standard blender and blend in batches). Add the cilantro and lime juice, cover, and blend until smooth. Season with additional salt, if needed. (The salsa can be covered and refrigerated for up to 5 days.)

Shallot-Honey Vinaigrette

This is the toss-together dressing to know, just vinegar, shallots, honey, and a little salt and pepper shaken with oil. It's a sure thing, whether you make it with pantry staples or see it as an opportunity to experiment (see Takeaways).

Makes about ¾ cup

⅔ cup neutral cooking oil (such as avocado or vegetable)

¼ cup apple cider vinegar

2 tablespoons minced shallot

1 tablespoon honey (such as wildflower)

¼ teaspoon kosher salt

⅛ teaspoon freshly ground black pepper

Combine the oil, vinegar, honey, shallot, salt, and pepper in a jar with a tight-fitting lid. Close the jar and shake the hell out of it to emulsify the dressing. (The dressing can be refrigerated in the jar for up to 5 days. Bring to room temperature and shake like hell again before using.)

TAKEAWAYS

- A neutral oil is my choice here because olive oil is too strong for me, but go with your favorite. Just remember to taste what you make and adjust elements to find the right balance. For example, if you use a nice extra virgin olive oil that's grassy and peppery, you might want to add more honey to mellow it or more vinegar to round out the richness. Try different oils—spicy to buttery—and build from there.
- Because the vinegar's flavor will be front and center, this dressing is your chance to experiment beyond the usual suspects. Moscatel vinegar is great for this, made from a dessert wine grape that adds soft, floral sweetness. Sherry vinegar or any white wine vinegar with a sweet touch will have the same effect.
- Another way to make this dressing your own is by adding your favorite chopped herbs (tarragon or chives are good).

Carrot-Top Green Goddess Dressing

What the fuck do you do with carrot tops? I had that thought enough times to try them in one of my favorite dressings. Because I hate wasting food, and because I like that specific vegetal flavor you get from stems and leafy parts. But carrots with tops can be harder to find, so in that case, use parsley. This is basically a mayo with lots of green stuff, and I use it as a dip as often as I put it on a salad.

Makes about 1 cup

½ cup coarsely chopped carrot tops and/or fresh parsley (leaves with some thin stems)

½ cup coarsely chopped scallions, white and green parts

1 clove garlic, peeled

1 large egg, at room temperature

2 teaspoons Dijon mustard

2 teaspoon fresh lemon juice

Kosher salt and freshly ground black pepper

¾ cup neutral cooking oil (such as avocado or vegetable)

Pulse the carrot tops, scallions, and garlic in a food processor until finely chopped. Add the egg, mustard, lemon juice, ¼ teaspoon salt, and ⅛ teaspoon pepper and pulse to combine. With the machine running, slowly add the oil through the feed tube. It should take about 30 seconds to add it all. Season with additional salt and pepper. (The dressing can be refrigerated in a covered container for up to 5 days.)

Cotija Dressing

Cotija cheese is a firm cow's milk cheese that crumbles easily, like feta in a lot of ways, but not as sharp. This thick and creamy dressing is best on sturdy greens like romaine, or on a wedge of iceberg (not to mention the Charred Broccolini on page 165).

Makes about 1⅓ cups

½ cup Mexican crema or sour cream

¼ cup crumbled cotija cheese

¼ cup unseasoned rice vinegar

1 clove garlic, crushed and mashed to a paste with a pinch of kosher salt

½ cup extra virgin olive oil

Kosher salt and freshly ground black pepper

Process the crema, cotija, rice vinegar, and garlic in a blender to combine. With the machine running, gradually pour in the oil and process until smooth. Season with salt and pepper. Transfer to a covered container and refrigerate until serving. (The dressing can be refrigerated for up to 5 days.)

TAKEAWAY

- You can buy cotija at Mexican markets and lots of supermarkets. Or sub feta, but keep in mind that imported varieties (made from goat's milk) will be tangier than domestic.

Green Ranch Dressing

Ranch gets a lot of shit—that happens sometimes when you're popular. But the haters can suck on this homemade take with a kick of herbs. It's a dressing, dip, sauce, and condiment. My best advice? Always use fresh herbs. Dried chives and dill don't give you the strong flavor you want in a dressing, and the fresh is what separates this ranch from the pack.

Makes about 1½ cups

1 cup sour cream

⅓ cup mayonnaise, preferably Kewpie

½ cup coarsely chopped fresh dill

¼ cup coarsely chopped chives or scallions (green parts only)

½ teaspoon garlic powder

½ teaspoon onion powder

½ teaspoon kosher salt

½ teaspoon freshly ground black pepper

2 tablespoons whole milk, as needed

In a medium bowl using an immersion blender, combine the sour cream, mayonnaise, dill, chives, garlic powder, onion powder, salt, and pepper. With the blender running, gradually add enough milk until the dressing is thick but pourable. Transfer to a covered container and refrigerate until serving. (The dressing can be refrigerated for up to 5 days.)

Homemade Chamoy

More and more, I'm leaning into the chamoy I grew up with in Mexican street food. It's a sweet, sour, spicy, salty condiment that's like the wild baby of fruit preserves and hot sauce. The base is pickled or dried fruit (I use apricots), and hibiscus flowers add a tart note against the easygoing heat of guajillo chiles. Use this bright red-orange topping as the beginnings of a barbecue sauce or the finish on Mango Sherbet (page 200).

Makes about 2½ cups

4 guajillo chiles, seeded and torn into large pieces

¾ cup sugar

¼ cup fresh lime juice

½ cup dried hibiscus flowers (flor de Jamaica)

1 cup loosely packed dried apricots, coarsely chopped

1 teaspoon kosher salt

Soak the chiles in hot tap water to cover in a small bowl until softened, about 20 minutes.

Meanwhile, bring 2 cups water, the sugar, and lime juice to a boil in a medium saucepan. Remove from the heat, add the hibiscus flowers, and let stand for 10 minutes to steep. Strain the hibiscus tea into a medium bowl, discarding the solids. Add the apricots and let stand for 5 minutes more. Pour into a blender.

Drain the guajillo, discarding the soaking liquid, and add to the blender along with the salt. Blend, with the lid ajar, until smooth. Taste the chamoy. If you want more heat, add cayenne pepper until you're happy. Let cool completely. (The chamoy can be refrigerated in a covered container for up to 1 month.)

Cranberry Sauce with Maple, Orange, and Thyme

This recipe isn't a knock on the loaf of cranberry gel that slides out of a can on Turkey Day. I'm into it, but sometimes the situation calls for something with flair. My version is almost as easy as opening a can, and it highlights the berry's tartness with rich maple, sweet citrus, and minty thyme for a taste that's familiar but fresh. Also, cranberry sauce is a great condiment whenever, on sandwiches and as an accent for meats.

Makes about 2½ cups

1 (12-ounce) bag fresh cranberries

Finely grated zest of 1 orange

1 cup fresh orange juice

1 cup maple sugar or packed light brown sugar

1 tablespoon fresh thyme leaves (no need to chop them)

Pinch of kosher salt

½ teaspoon pure maple extract (optional)

½ teaspoon vanilla extract

Bring the cranberries, orange zest, orange juice, maple sugar, thyme, and salt to a boil in a medium saucepan over high heat, stirring to dissolve the sugar. Reduce the heat to medium-low and cook at a brisk simmer, stirring occasionally, until all the cranberries have burst and the juices have thickened, about 15 minutes. Stir in the maple extract (if using) and the vanilla. Let cool completely. (The sauce can be refrigerated in a covered container for up to 1 month.)

TAKEAWAY

- Thanks to the acidity of the sugar and berries, cranberry sauce keeps forever, so make it well ahead for a holiday meal. It's one less thing to do when you're dealing with a big menu.

Caramel Sauce

If you want to win at dessert, you should know how to whip up a caramel sauce. It's not as hard as it looks on TV. I've been asked the "secret" to caramel. It's waiting. That's it. It's a very easy thing, just don't be weird. Stop touching the pan and let the thing cook! I tend to have ingredients on hand, so it can be ready in under 10 minutes. Don't be afraid of the caramel, especially when it starts smoking. That's your sign that the syrup is ready.

Makes about 1¾ cups

1¼ cups granulated sugar

1 cup heavy cream, heated to lukewarm

2 tablespoons unsalted butter

1 teaspoon vanilla extract

Large pinch of flaky salt

Put the sugar in a medium saucepan and pour in ¼ cup water. Bring to a boil over high heat. Cover tightly and cook for 3 minutes. Uncover and cook, without stirring but occasionally swirling the saucepan by the handle, until the caramel is dark amber and gives off a little smoke, 4 to 5 minutes. (Judge the caramel with your senses, not a timer. It should have a slightly acrid smell, too, but not burned.) Remove from the heat.

Gradually (it foams up like crazy) stir in the cream. Return to very low heat and stir until all the caramel is dissolved. Add the butter and whisk until absorbed. Whisk in the vanilla. Remove from the heat and let cool. Serve warm with the pinch of flaky salt. (The caramel sauce can be cooled completely and stored in an airtight container for up to 2 weeks. Reheat until pourable before serving, either in a small saucepan over low heat or in the microwave on medium power in short bursts, stirring often until smooth.)

Candied Hazelnuts and Hazelnut Syrup

This is a cool kitchen trick where you get two great ingredients for the price of one. The hazelnut syrup is nice to have handy for stirring into coffee (or try the Hazelnut Coffee Soda on page 216). And if you don't eat them all as a snack in one sitting, use the hazelnuts in salads.

Makes about 1 cup candied hazelnuts and about 1 cup hazelnut syrup

1 cup hazelnuts

1 cup sugar

Flaky salt (optional)

To roast and skin the hazelnuts, preheat the oven to 350°F. Spread the hazelnuts on a large baking sheet. Bake, stirring occasionally, until the skins are split and the flesh underneath is browning, about 10 minutes. Wrap the nuts in a kitchen towel and let cool until easy to handle, 15 to 20 minutes. Using the towel, rub the nuts to remove most of the skins. Don't worry if some of the skin stays attached.

Bring the sugar and 1 cup water to a boil over high heat, stirring to dissolve the sugar. Add the nuts and reduce the heat to medium. Cook at a brisk simmer until the syrup reduces by about one-fourth, 15 to 20 minutes. Remove from the heat and let stand for 10 minutes. Strain through a wire sieve set over a bowl, reserving the nuts and the syrup. Let cool completely. Transfer the syrup to a jar or covered container. (The syrup can be refrigerated for up to 3 weeks.)

Spread the hazelnuts on a silicone mat or parchment paper. Sprinkle with flaky salt, if using. Let cool completely, then break apart the nuts to separate them. (The hazelnuts can be stored in an airtight container at room temperature for up to 2 months.)

Flaky Pastry Dough

I hate it when dough cracks. So it needs to be easy to roll, and that is all about the ingredients and how you treat those ingredients, both with your hands and with temperature. You also want your crust to be flaky and crisp but tender, with that strong butter flavor. I taught a lot of pie classes at Seattle's Hot Stove Society, and all my tips and tricks for clutch crust are here. This dough works for large and small batches, and sweet and savory baking—everything from empanadas and pot pie to my Balsamic Berry Slab Pie (page 203).

Makes enough dough for
2 (9-inch) pie shells or
1 (13x9-inch) slab pie

3 cups unbleached all-purpose flour, plus more for shaping

½ teaspoon kosher salt

1¼ cups (2½ sticks) cold unsalted butter, cut into ½-inch cubes

⅓ cup plus 1 tablespoon ice water, as needed

2 tablespoons unseasoned rice vinegar

Mix the flour and salt together in a medium bowl. Add the butter and mix to coat the individual cubes with flour. Using your fingers, squish the cubes into flat flakes, being sure to flatten them all. The mixture should look crumbly with about half being larger flakes.

Combine the ice water and vinegar. Gradually add the liquid to the flour mixture, stirring with a fork to distribute it throughout, until the dough clumps together. You may not need all the liquid, or you may need to add a tablespoon or so additional ice water. Gather up the dough into a mass. It should hold together like Play-Doh.

Turn out the dough onto a lightly floured work surface. For two pies or empanadas, divide the dough in half. For a slab pie, divide the dough into two portions, one slightly larger than the other. Flatten each portion into a thick rectangle. (For round pies, shape into two disks.) Wrap in plastic wrap and refrigerate until chilled, at least 30 minutes or up to 2 days.

Small-Batch Flaky Pastry Dough:

Use 1½ cups flour, ¼ teaspoon salt, 10 tablespoons cold unsalted butter, ¼ cup ice water, and 1 tablespoon rice vinegar. Shape the final dough into one flat disk, wrap, and chill.

TAKEAWAYS

- Some recipes use shortening or lard in addition to, or in place of, the butter. These two fats have less water than butter does, and too much water can react with the flour's gluten to make tough crust. Therefore, pie doughs that include them are flakier. But for my money, nothing beats the flavor of butter. The trick is how the butter is handled. You gotta leave the butter in large flakes in the dough. When it melts in the oven, it creates steam to puff the dough into thin, distinct layers. If the butter is fully incorporated into the dough (it will look crumbly without any flakes), the resulting crust will be more cookie-like than flaky.
- I like using my fingers to squeeze the butter into the dough because I can feel its progress. However, you can make the entire dough in a stand mixer fitted with the paddle attachment on *low* speed. The speed is important, or the flour will kick up out of the bowl. Be sure to mix just until the butter flakes are about the size of marbles, no more. When adding the liquid, do not overmix—as soon as the dough clumps, stop mixing.
- If this dough has a secret ingredient, it's rice vinegar. The acidity relaxes the gluten in the flour for tenderness and easy rolling.
- All the dough ingredients should be cold. For best results, freeze the flour 30 minutes or so to chill it.
- Conversely, the dough should only chill 30 to 60 minutes in the fridge if you want it to roll out without cracking. If it chills longer and feels hard, whack the wrapped dough with the rolling pin a few times to soften before working it.

No-Knead Pizza Dough

This dough may be a slow riser, but that's why it has superior flavor and texture. It's super-easy and takes no kneading. Don't let the rising time stop you, as it can sit at room temperature all day if you make it in the morning to use that night. The dough is used in my Italian Grandma Pizza on page 124 and the soft pretzels on page 30.

Makes enough dough for 1 (18x13-inch) pizza

4 cups unbleached all-purpose flour

1 cup semolina or yellow cornmeal, plus more for sprinkling

1 teaspoon instant yeast

5 teaspoons kosher salt

½ cup extra virgin olive oil, plus more for the pan

2 tablespoons honey

Mix the flour, semolina, yeast, and salt in a large bowl that will contain the dough when tripled. Make a well in the center and pour in 1¾ cups water, the oil, and honey and stir with a silicone spatula to make a shaggy, sticky dough.

Hold the dough at the 12 o'clock position and pull it up about your palm's length without tearing and fold it over into the center. Repeat the stretching and folding at the 3, 6, and 9 o'clock positions and the dough will smooth out. Repeat, if you wish. Scrape down the sides of the bowl. Shape the dough into a ball. Drizzle the top with oil and turn the dough over to give it a light coating.

Cover the bowl tightly with plastic wrap and let stand at room temperature until tripled in volume, at least 8 hours or up to 12. (After 12 hours, you can refrigerate the dough for up to 3 days.) Let the chilled dough stand in a warm place for 2 to 3 hours before stretching.

TAKEAWAYS

- A no-knead dough works because it has a high ratio of liquid to flour. The liquid activates the gluten in the flour just like kneading. But the key is time—let the dough rise for at least 8 hours, though I like to refrigerate for 2 or 3 days to give it a sourdough taste. You bread bakers out there know how time makes all the difference, because it gives the enzymes in the flour time to develop flavor.

- It's important that the dough is at room temperature before stretching. Cold dough will fight it and retract. Don't worry—the dough will rise again during the warm-up period.

Acknowledgments

First and foremost, I need to thank **Grand**. You taught me to dance in the kitchen. And you showed me that cooking isn't just about feeding people—it's about joy, rhythm, and love in every movement.

Endless thanks to **my ma and my family** for raising me with so much love and instilling in me the belief that anything is possible. That foundation has carried me through every kitchen, every challenge, and every dream I've chased.

To my beautiful girlfriend, **Jenn Cho**, you inspire me every day. Your support, creativity, and belief in me mean more than I can put into words.

To my chef and mentor, **Nate Crave**, thank you for showing me how to make food fucking nice. You taught me the details matter, the craft matters, and that pushing yourself is always worth it.

Chef **Dezi Bonow**, thank you for hiring me at my first Seattle kitchen job, and for inspiring me way beyond it. Many thanks to chef **Ron Anderson** for always telling me to ride the wave, and to chef **Joe Labatt** for telling me to go all in on this social media thing.

Tom Douglas Restaurants basically raised me through my entire 20s. Those kitchens and people shaped the cook I am today, and I owe them forever.

To my cat, **Ladybird**, for always being by my side in the kitchen at home. You've been my quiet companion through recipe testing, late-night editing, and everything in between.

To my insanely talented writer, **Erin Ryan**, thank you for absolutely crushing this book. You took my ideas, my chaos, and my voice, and put them on the page with precision and soul. And to **Rick Rodgers**, the recipe whisperer and detail king. You spent months testing, reworking, and making sense of my notes—dedication that made this book solid and truly cookable. Together, you two got the puzzle pieces to fit.

To my incredible photographer, **Sarah Flotard**—not only are you stunning and ridiculously talented, but you were the one who first put a real camera in my hands back in 2015, teaching me how to shoot food on the rooftop of my South Lake Union apartment. I couldn't imagine anyone else bringing these recipes to life.

To **the entire production team**—especially **Callie Meyer** on food and prop styling—you worked your asses off to capture my food the way I see it, and I can't thank you enough.

To my good friend **Pete Taylor**, founder of Spiceology—during one of the most uncertain times of my life, when restaurants were shutting down because of COVID, you took me in and made me the sole content creator for Spiceology. That opportunity was the springboard to what I do today, and I'll always be grateful for it.

Joanne Molinaro—the Korean Vegan—you are such an inspiration. You're the one who pushed me to make my own cookbook, and without you, this wouldn't exist. You lit the spark and gave me the courage to run with it.

To my publisher, **Simon Element**, thank you for giving me the chance to share my food in a different and wonderful way. S&S is one of the greats, and it's an honor to have your mark on my book. To **Doris Cooper**, my editor, I could tell from our first meeting that you knew your shit, and I appreciate the direction you gave my vision.

To **Charlie Brotherstone**, the most badass book agent ever, thank you for believing in me, fighting for me, and making sure this thing came to life the right way.

To my mentor, **Benji Travis**—in this mysterious, ever-changing world of YouTube, you've always been a source of wisdom, clarity, and sanity. I've learned so much from you.

To **Olivia Miller**, my partner at YouTube, and to **YouTube** itself—without this platform, I wouldn't be doing this (I have the YouTube logo tattooed on my ankle to prove it). Thanks also to my TikTok manager, **Melissa Tecson**, and my Instagram savior, **CJ Hernandez**.

To my manager and best friend, **Victoria Wright**—if it weren't for you, I'd be fucked. You've been with me through every high, every low, every big swing, and every crazy idea. I couldn't do this without you.

Leslie Kelly, you are a great writer and person, and I'll never forget how cool it was to be named The Most Fun Chef to Watch on TikTok by *Forbes*.

I'm constantly learning and upping my game because I'm surrounded by amazing friends who also happen to be the best creators and chefs. There are way too many to name them all, but special shout-outs go to **Sulhee Jessica Woo**, **Jon Kung, Shota Nakajima**, **Chris Cho**, **Max Grebb**, **Adam Witt**, **Matt Groark**, **Noah Sims**, **Akshay Bhardwaj**, **Lisa Nguyen**, **Jeanelle Castro**, and **Doug Libby**.

To **my subscribers**, and to anyone who's ever watched my videos, cooked my recipes, or tried my food at a pop-up—thank you. You've given me the kind of support and connection I never dreamed possible, and you're as much a part of this book as I am.

And finally, to everyone who's ever cooked a meal with me, eaten my food, or helped me find my way on this wild journey, this book is for you.

About the Author

Matthew Norman Broussard fell in love with cooking ever since his Grand taught him how to cook an egg. After learning the basics at Le Cordon Bleu and a handful of Texas restaurants, he made his mark in Seattle with the Tom Douglas Restaurants family.

Matthew documented his cooking online, and it took off like wildfire, leading him down the rabbit hole of opportunity—cooking with one of his heroes, Marcus Samuelsson; doing pop-ups with The French Laundry Culinary Garden (and hundreds of others across the country); being named the most fun chef to watch on TikTok by *Forbes*; grilling for the NFL's official Super Bowl tailgate. Sharing his stories and his food, @acooknamedmatt has drawn billions of views across his platforms, but more importantly, he has connected with people everywhere.

He is inspired by his cat Ladybird, eating good Szechuan food with his girlfriend, Pokémon cards, and long walks that include finding the perfect spoon at a thrift store. He also cringes at writing about himself in the third person, but here we are.

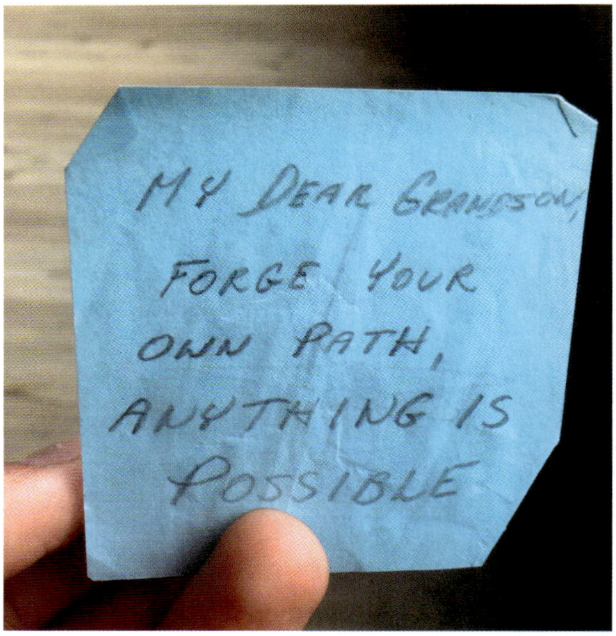
MY DEAR GRANDSON,
FORGE YOUR
OWN PATH,
ANYTHING IS
POSSIBLE

Index

SIMON ELEMENT
An Imprint of Simon & Schuster, LLC
1230 Avenue of the Americas
New York, NY 10020

First Simon Element hardcover edition August 2026

SIMON ELEMENT and colophon are registered trademarks of Simon & Schuster, LLC

Simon & Schuster strongly believes in freedom of expression and stands against censorship in all its forms. For more information, visit BooksBelong.com.

For information about special discounts for bulk purchases, please contact Simon & Schuster Special Sales at 1-866-506-1949 or business@simonandschuster.com.

The Simon & Schuster Speakers Bureau can bring authors to your live event. For more information or to book an event, contact the Simon & Schuster Speakers Bureau at 1-866-248-3049 or visit our website at www.simonspeakers.com.

Interior design by Jose Fernandez

Manufactured in Canada

10 9 8 7 6 5 4 3 2 1

Library of Congress Control Number: 2026936635

ISBN 978-1-6680-7714-6
ISBN 978-1-6680-7715-3 (ebook)

Scan here to get book recommendations, exclusive offers, and more delivered to your inbox.